FRESH GROWN

FRESH GROWN

HOW TO USE, STORE, + MAKE THE
MOST OF YOUR VEGETABLES

Andrea Kristin

GREY ARROW PRESS

PUBLISHING

GREY ARROW PRESS
PUBLISHING

This book was written, photographed, illustrated, and designed by Andrea Kristin.

FIRST EDITION
Photography by Andrea Kristin
Photography (pg 10, 16) by Denis Forstbauer
Photography (pg 19) by Jessica Musslewhite
Photography (pg 320) by Tracey Crown

Published by Grey Arrow Press
Made in Canada
ISBN 978-1-0688109-2-3 (Electronic book)
ISBN 978-1-0688109-1-6 (Paperback)
ISBN 978-1-0688109-0-9 (Hardcover)

FRESH GROWN. Copyright © 2024 by Andrea Kristin. All rights reserved. No part of this book may be reproduced in any form without written permission from the publisher.

For more information, please visit greyarrowpress.ca

To Denis and our kids,
for the beautiful life we've built together.
I love you.

FOR THE

veggie lover + veggie curious

and anyone wanting to explore

the world of fresh grown.

ROOTS
page 91

STEMS
page 133

LEAVES
page 175

BULBS
page 213

FLOWERS
page 225

FRUITS
page 245

SEEDS
page 289

CONTENTS

Welcome..................................11
The Root Of It.........................15
It Started From Scratch............ 17

APPRECIATING YOUR VEGETABLES
Garden To Plate.....................22
Eating Seasonally..................25

BRINGING HOME VEGETABLES
Living Organisms...................28
First Things First...................31
Storing Your Cured Vegetables......33
Kitchen Tips..........................34

MAKING THEM LAST
Eat Them All Year..................44
Freezing Your Vegetables.........47
Canning Your Vegetables.........53
Dehydrating Your Vegetables....61
Fermenting Your Vegetables....71
Pickling Your Vegetables.........77

VEGETABLE PAGES

Growing Forward...................317
Vegetable Index...................318

RECIPES
Roasted Vegetables..................37
Garden Pesto...........................39
Vegetable Purées.....................41
Vegetable Broth......................59
Seasoning Mix.........................67
Classic Pickle..........................80
Quick Pickle............................81
Pickling Liquid Salad Dressing.....85
Perfect Pumpkin Purée.............267

9

WELCOME

As I write this book, I am snacking on a crisp garden carrot. The sun shines brightly through my kitchen window and casts a golden glow across the table while I battle its glare on my laptop screen. Outside, we are in the throes of harvest season on the farm. Denis and the crew are working hard to bring the remaining vegetables into storage before the heavy frost comes and shuts our market garden down for the winter.

Farming is so seasonal. Eating from a garden is so seasonal. During the summer here in Central Alberta, we grow a delicious variety of produce in our market garden. We all feel rich from it. And then our six months of northern winter hits and eating local grown becomes about digging into our reserves (storage, pantry, and freezer) to keep enjoying whatever garden pleasures we were able to save.

It's been a learning curve for me, dealing with this wide variety and seasonal influx of fresh vegetables. Wanting to feed my family wholesome, nutritious food and learn how to make good use of our bounty, it has taken me years to gain all the knowledge and experience I am excited to share with you here. I hope this book will be a valuable resource for you (as it is for me) — a guide to vegetable usage, an inspiration, and a solid, practical starting point to build your creativity. So here we go.

THE ROOT OF IT

When Denis and I started our organic market garden farm with our five kiddos in tow, we were excited to grow a bounty of wonderful produce for our local community. Ordering our first seeds had us dreaming about all of the exciting items we would produce. We couldn't wait to hold the vegetables in our hands, taste the flavours, and share the harvest with our customers to enjoy around their dinner tables. Farm-to-fork deliciousness had begun. Our community was enthusiastic, and our CSA program was a smashing success.

Over the years, as we expanded our program, continued to grow a wide variety of vegetables, and fed hundreds of returning customers, we noticed a few recurring themes. Number one, although our customers loved their fresh produce and were excited by the incredible variety ("it's like Christmas in a box each week!"), encountering new vegetables was daunting for them. And number two, they wanted guidance from us on how to fully use, store, enjoy, and make the most of their abundance of fresh vegetables.

The most frequent questions we get asked as market garden farmers are:
+ What is this?
+ How do I eat this? (Are all these parts edible?)
+ What sort of things can I make with this?
+ How do you store this to keep it fresh?
+ What can I do with my excess vegetables piling up in my refrigerator?
+ How can I preserve my vegetables to last through the year?

I wrote this book to answer all these questions and be a comprehensive guide for you to fully use and enjoy all your delicious, nutritious veggies.

IT STARTED FROM SCRATCH

I wasn't always passionate about vegetables. My first memorable encounter with fresh vegetables was the evening Denis (the cute guy I had been dating for a couple of months) first brought me to visit his family's farm. I was 17 at the time. Growing up in the suburbs, my only experience with produce up to that point was a few staples from the supermarket and frozen foods section. We had no garden and no real produce variety in my childhood home. Our family dinners involved the classics— carrots, potatoes, frozen peas, and the odd green salad thrown in for good measure. Farmers markets and CSAs were completely foreign to me; fresh was not something I thought about, and I had never seen or heard of most of the vegetables in this book.

It was a warm, sunny evening as 19-year-old Denis drove me through the agricultural landscape in his bright red compact car. Pulling into the gravel driveway of his parents' property, we parked next to a large, weathered, white barn. Hopping out of the vehicle, we were met by a few of his brothers coming in from the field with dirt on their hands and grins on their faces. It was an expansive, hundred-acre, organic vegetable farm that his parents had started from scratch and that he and his siblings grew up cultivating. There was so much pride in him around it and a real passion for the produce they grew. It lit me up to see the enthusiasm sparking in him to show me all of it, and I couldn't wait to discover this unique world that made him tick so vibrantly.

After enjoying an energetic outdoor supper with everyone back at the house, Denis invited me for a stroll to see the garden.
    "Kick off your shoes," he said, tossing his own aside. We proceeded to walk barefoot through the acres of dirt and lush growth.

The sun was beginning to set behind the surrounding mountains, bathing the whole valley in a golden glow. The birds were chirping and flying overhead as he took my hand. I gazed in wonder as he proudly named the different kinds of plants. I thought he was teasing me when he pointed and told me the kale was something to eat. (That dark green, weird, leafy thing? That surely couldn't be food!) I look back and laugh now, but it was just so far from my food experience at the time.

I remember when he bent down to the damp earth, pulled a handful of carrots from the soil, and wiped the dirt from them with the old T-shirt he was wearing. Then he handed me one to munch on as we continued talking. It tasted incredibly crunchy and sweet— far better than anything I'd ever eaten from a grocery store. I was caught up in wonderment. What was this incredible lifestyle?

I will never forget the next moment when he plunged his fist deep into the earth, pulled out a raw potato, and gave me a wink before biting into it like an apple. Who was this guy? What was this life he lived? Later on, I learned that farmers don't actually eat raw potatoes like apples (and truthfully, neither did he— it had been a one-time move for my benefit. Such a charmer.)— but it had worked. I was hooked. Over the next decade, as we fell in love and began building our own life together, the call back to farming and that joy of fresh vegetables was never far from our hearts.

A decade and a half later, with five kids and one province over, we purchased a little slice of paradise and started our own organic vegetable farm affectionately known as Grey Arrow Farm. On our acreage, we grow delicious, wholesome food for our community— over 50 types of vegetables and herbs over 2.5 acres of garden— which we sell to folks mainly through our CSA (veggie box subscription) program. It's been an incredible journey, and we love our continually growing community of CSA members and veggie-passionate folks who participate with our farm.

I have come a long way from my wide-eyed, veggie-virgin roots. I've stretched myself and discovered ways to cook and enjoy our wealth of produce while keeping things practical and doable for our busy family of seven. I am excited to share with you everything I've learned over these past 20 years on how to use, enjoy, and maximize all your fresh vegetables. And while I'm not going to have you try eating your potatoes raw (unless you have someone to impress!), I am going to share all the tips and tricks I've gleaned along the way to enjoy every last bit of your delicious seasonal produce.

So let's dive in.

APPRECIATING YOUR VEGETABLES

From garden to plate

GARDEN TO PLATE

Whether you think about it or not, vegetables probably make an appearance in some form on your daily dinner table. They add colour, texture, and flavour to meals. They take you on culinary adventures. They tell the story of your region.

Not only do these earthy edibles add vibrance to our lives, but they also provide us with health, well-being, and sustenance. Vegetables are a vitally important staple for human existence, supplying a wide range of the nutrients we need for our bodies to function. They also provide us with energy and hydration while preventing disease, illness, and deterioration— that's going far beyond being markers of simple food and flavour. Vegetables are a big deal.

There are thousands of different vegetable varieties worldwide, from edible roots to stems to fruits to leaves and beyond. Every country and region boasts its own unique produce based on what is possible to grow in the local climate and geography. Though this book focuses on the produce we grow here in Canada, most of these items are known and grown in many parts of the world and enjoyed across many cultures.

The best nourishment comes from regularly enjoying a wide variety and colourful assortment of vegetables in your diet. The more vegetables you eat, the better off you are. May this book help you thoroughly enjoy and make the most of all the tasty produce available to you. Welcome to the wonderful world of vegetables.

EATING SEASONALLY

Seasonal eating is the concept of eating foods that are ripe and in season in your local area. It involves eating locally grown produce as much as possible because it is fresher, tastier, and more nutritious than food consumed out of season (e.g. produce available year-round at your local grocery store that had to be transported from thousands of kilometres away).

Out-of-season produce found at your local supermarket had to be harvested BEFORE it was ripe to be shipped and distributed to your local retail store without going bad along the way. Produce grown locally, on the other hand, is allowed to fully mature and sun ripen before it is picked and handed to you (not having to travel distances or sit in stores for any period of time), so it yields its best flavour as well as higher nutrient content, giving you maximum taste and nutritional benefits.

Seasonal eating also invites you to expand your vegetable repertoire. Veggie variety is vital for the body to get all the essential nutrients it needs. Each type of vegetable boasts its own set of benefits to you with its body-boosting vitamins, minerals, fibre, antioxidants, and the like. When shopping at the grocery store, most of us have our comfort zone of familiar veggies that we stick to, the ones we are used to regularly eating and cooking with. Eating seasonally, however, requires you to branch out and enjoy whatever produce is ripe and available in your local climate, embracing your region's diverse and delicious offerings. Seasonal eating is incredibly beneficial and a flavourful adventure.

BRINGING HOME VEGETABLES

Keeping that produce fresh

LIVING ORGANISMS

Once plants and vegetables are picked, they begin the natural process of breaking down- some much faster than others. Refrigeration helps to slow down those natural processes that cause spoilage so you can continue to get the most life out of your fresh produce.

You'll notice early on that some vegetables have a longer shelf life while others go bad more quickly. As a basic rule of thumb, tender leafy greens have the shortest shelf life (5-7 days), while root vegetables and cured items (such as onions and garlic) can last for months on end. Most produce items fall somewhere in the middle, lasting a couple of weeks when properly stored, but will keep up to 12 months once frozen or preserved.

There are many ways to extend the life of your produce, whether you are struggling to get through it all during the week, trying to stockpile a garden haul for the winter, or simply wanting to enjoy your delicious veggies all year round. Throughout these pages, I will walk you through various ways of storing, preserving and prolonging the shelf life of your items so you can more fully enjoy whatever produce you've got.

FIRST THINGS FIRST

General guidelines for keeping your fresh produce fresh.
Keep in mind each item is unique. You can look up individual vegetables in these pages to learn their specific fresh storage instructions.

GIVE THEM A RINSE

Most farms + gardens do an initial wash of your produce before delivery, however, to keep it crisp and enlivened, give it a rinse before refrigerating.

NOTE: Some items should **not** be rinsed before refrigerating such as beans, peas, cabbage, onions, zucchini, summer squash, and cured vegetables.

SEPARATE TOPS FROM VEGGIES

Always separate the leafy tops from veggies (carrots, beets, radishes, etc.) before storing, as they pull moisture out of the vegetable.

NOTE: Many tops are edible and can be consumed too (see individual vegetable pages). Both parts should be stored separately in order to remain fresh longest.

REFRIGERATE IN SEALED BAGS OR CONTAINERS

The best way to store fresh garden produce is in sealable, reusable plastic bags or containers. Rinsing and sealing help keep the produce crisp and prevent it from going limp.

STORING YOUR CURED VEGETABLES

Cured items will come to you later in the season, in the fall. These include onions, potatoes, garlic, and winter squash that have developed a hardy outer skin and are ready to be stored in a cool, dark, dry place rather than the refrigerator.

During the summer, the onions you receive will be fresh, not cured (with their green tops still attached), and the potatoes will be new (still with their thin, tender skin). These should be refrigerated. Later on in the season, however, these items will come to you with a hardy, dry outer skin, ready to be stored elsewhere.

Cured items like it dry, cool, and dark and will last for months if you can accommodate this. Think darkened pantry, basement storage room, cold storage, or garage.

Do not store these guys in plastic bags (unless they have holes for ventilation); use paper bags, baskets, or bins without lids so the air can circulate around them in storage. Do not store onions directly next to your potatoes either, as they will cause premature spoilage (a few feet away is fine).

Kitchen Tips

MY STAPLE KITCHEN ITEMS

These are my must-have kitchen items for dealing with fresh produce:

- vegetable peeler
- a good knife + cutting board
- large sealable, reusable plastic bags (I always have a stash of these on hand to store produce items in the refrigerator and freezer)
- large stockpot (for making broth, canning, and large batches of soup to freeze)
- box grater (to shred vegetables for coleslaws, salads, fermenting, and baking).
- food processor (for making veggie purées, sauces, dressings, dips)

SCRAP BOWL

When working with veggies, keep a spare bowl handy to collect all of the veggie scraps along the way. This makes for an easy and efficient way to keep things tidy in the kitchen when cooking and makes for one quick dump at the end to transfer all scraps to the compost.

SCRAPS FOR BROTH

Save and freeze your ends and peels for added flavour and nutrition in your soup broths. (See page 59)

BATCH PREP

Certain items can be prepped ahead (even the day you bring them home) to make for easy grab-and-go use in your meals throughout the week. Here are my favourite prep-ahead tips for simplifying veggie eating.

PREP AHEAD TIPS

- Kale -
Strip leaves from stems. Discard stems, chop leaves, and pack tightly in a sealed bag in refrigerator ready for use.

- Beets -
Remove tops and batch boil whole beets (pg 94). Peel once cooled. Store in refrigerator, ready for use in salads, sides, or baking.

- Pumpkin or Winter Squash -
Bake whole and purée (pg 267). Store in refrigerator, ready for pies, pancakes, and fall baking.

- Greens + Tops -
Make a ready-to-go greens mix for easy salads, sautées, casseroles, or omelets. Strip leaves from stems with your edible tops (beet, turnip, radish, etc.) or leafy greens. Tear leaves to your desired size and pack them in a sealed bag in the refrigerator for easy use.

- Salad Dressing -
Make a large jar of your favourite salad dressing. Store in refrigerator for easy use throughout the week with your fresh produce.

ROASTED VEGETABLES

This is my favourite way to cook vegetables. Roasting vegetables caramelizes their natural sugars, intensifying the flavour and creating a slightly sweet, nutty taste. This method is simple and delicious and can be done with virtually any vegetable (fresh or frozen). It makes them crisp on the outside and tender on the inside. Roasting also preserves more of their nutrients than boiling or steaming (where some vitamins and minerals leach out into the water). Enjoy them as a side or added to salads or grain bowls.

Vegetable/s of choice (such as potatoes, carrots, cauliflower, onions, etc.)
Olive oil
Salt and pepper (to taste)
Optional: herbs and spices (such as rosemary, thyme, paprika, garlic powder, etc.) or seasoning mix

Preheat your oven to 425°F
Chop the vegetables into uniform-sized pieces to ensure even cooking. Larger pieces will take longer to cook; smaller ones will cook more quickly.

In a large bowl, toss the vegetables with oil until evenly coated. (Don't overdo it with the oil; you want just enough to give a light glossy coating so the vegetables crisp up.) Season with salt and pepper (you can always add more after cooking if needed). Add any additional herbs, spices or seasonings you like.

Spread the vegetables in a single layer on a baking sheet. Place in oven, roasting until the vegetables are fork tender and caramelized, tossing once or twice for even cooking. (Cook time will vary depending on the type and size of the vegetables, but it is typically between 25-45 minutes.) Serve warm.

MAKES 2 CUPS

GARDEN PESTO

A great way to use up your extra summer greens and enjoy bright summer flavours year round. Pesto freezes well, making this a common garden item we enjoy in our meals throughout the year.

2 cups packed, chopped fresh greens (such as those listed below)
1/4 cup nuts (pine nuts, walnuts, pecans, almonds, cashews, pumpkin seeds, sunflower seeds)

1/2 cup extra virgin olive oil
2 cloves garlic (or garlic scapes), minced
1/2 cup grated parmesan
1/4 teaspoon salt (more to taste)
Juice of half a lemon (optional)

Basil
Beet Greens
Carrot Tops
Cilantro
Garlic Scapes
Kale
Kohlrabi Leaves
Parsley
Radish Tops
Spinach
Swiss Chard
Turnip Tops

Place all ingredients in a small food processor. Pulse until blended. Season with salt to taste.

Store in sealed jar or container in refrigerator for up to a week, or freezer for up to a year.

NOTE: When freezing your pesto, remember to leave 1" of headspace to allow for expansion.

OUR FAVOURITE PESTO USES:
Pizza Sauce | Grilled Cheese | Soup Topper | Pasta Sauce | Warm Potato Salad Dressing

VEGETABLE PURÉES

Purées offer you further ways to enjoy your produce. Incorporate them into baking (muffins, cakes, pancakes) or to add flavourful creaminess and nutrition to soups, sauces, dips and spreads. It simply involves cooking the vegetable until tender and blending it to a smooth consistency. Purées also freeze well for use throughout the year.

Vegetable/s of choice

Wash and peel the vegetables as needed. Chop them loosely into evenly sized-pieces.

Cook until tender using your preferred cooking method (boiling, steaming, roasting, or microwaving). Once the vegetables are cooked and tender, transfer them to a blender or food processor. Blend until smooth, scraping down the sides. Add reserved cooking liquid or water as needed to achieve your desired consistency.

If freezing, scoop purée into containers or freezer bags in pre-portioned amounts (such as 1 cup or 2 cups) based on what you plan to use it for. This will make it much easier when thawing for later use.

For pumpkin and squash purée, see pg 267

MAKING THEM LAST

Extending their natural shelf life

EAT THEM ALL YEAR

There are many ways to keep your vegetables well past their natural expiration date. Whether you are looking to stockpile large quantities of produce for the winter or simply wish not to waste your lonely parsnip in the back of the refrigerator— all these options will allow you to extend the life of whatever you've got. Each method is more doable than you might think.

Ways to preserve produce:

FREEZING

CANNING

DEHYDRATING

FERMENTING

PICKLING

I'll walk you through each of these methods and how to get started with them. You can then take and run with them as far or as little as you want. With a bit of intention, you can keep enjoying those seasonal flavours and nutrients even in the off-season.

FREEZING YOUR VEGETABLES

Freezing halts those natural processes that cause spoilage so you can continue to enjoy your produce and its nutritional benefits well past its season.

There are three ways to freeze your vegetables:

RAW + BLANCHED + COOKED

All three methods work great, though certain vegetables will stand up better under one or the other. See individual vegetable pages for specific freezing instructions.

The benefit of raw freezing is that it takes no time at all. Blanching requires a few more steps but can help retain more of the vegetable colour and texture and prolong its freezer shelf life. The benefit of freezing pre-cooked vegetables and foods is that they take no time to prepare later on; they just need to be thawed and reheated.

Properly frozen produce can maintain good quality for up to 12 months. After that, it remains safe to eat, but the quality and nutritional value will begin to decline.

RAW FREEZING

With this method, the peeled, chopped, or shredded vegetable goes directly to the freezer (in a sealed bag or container) without any cooking or preparation first. This method is quick and simple and all that is necessary for many vegetables. However, others will become mealy or mushy after thawing if they haven't been blanched first. Be sure to look at the individual vegetable pages for specific freezing instructions.

BLANCHED FREEZING

Blanching is a short-cooking method where the peeled, chopped vegetable is immersed in boiling water for a couple of minutes (depending on the size), then quickly removed and submerged into ice water to stop the cooking process before heading to the freezer. This method can help the vegetable retain more of its flavour, vibrant colour and texture and extend its freezer shelf life. Some items are essential to blanch before freezing, while others are completely fine frozen raw. Check the individual vegetable pages for specific freezing instructions.

STEP-BY-STEP FOR BLANCHING

1. Bring a large pot of water to a rolling boil. Prepare a large bowl of ice water.

2. Submerge the vegetables in the boiling water and start a timer.

3. Boil for 2 minutes unless otherwise recommended for that vegetable (see vegetable pages).

4. Using a slotted spoon or tongs, quickly transfer the blanched vegetables to a bowl of ice water.

5. Allow the vegetables to cool in the ice water for the same amount of time they were blanched.

6. Remove the vegetables from the ice water and drain them well before using or preserving them.

COOKED FREEZING

Whether it's plain cooked vegetables, veggie purée for later use in baking or sauces, or a pre-made soup, stew, or casserole ready to heat and serve for a coming meal, freezing pre-cooked food can be super handy. It requires more time upfront to prepare, but is a time-saver later on when all that's needed is thawing and reheating for a tasty home-cooked meal.

Once frozen, vegetables are no longer ideal for salads, snacking, or raw use as they lose their crispness. However, they are still great for cooked options (such as soups, stews, casseroles, sauces, gratins, and baking) or smoothies.

Freezing Tips

TRAY FREEZE FIRST

If you don't want individual pieces to freeze together into one giant clump, you can tray freeze them first. Spread pieces in a single layer on a parchment-lined baking sheet or shallow dish and place them in the freezer for an hour until they are semi-frozen before transferring to freezer bags or sealed containers.

LEAVE HEADSPACE

Always leave a little space at the top of the bag or container (1/2" to 1" is recommended) to allow for expansion.

PREPARE AHEAD

Consider what produce preparations might be most practical and useful for you. Freeze cooked puréed vegetables for use in your baking or sauces later on. Sauté a veggie medley and freeze it to add to stews or casseroles. Or make a big old batch of soup, stew, or casserole to freeze for pre-made meals down the road.

TO USE

Frozen produce items can be added directly to your cooking, there is no need to thaw before use.

PRE-PORTION IT

I recommend freezing your shredded or puréed vegetables in pre-portioned amounts based on what you want to use them for (perhaps 1 cup or 2 cup portions, or even smaller amounts like ice cube trays for tomato paste or chopped herbs in oil) before transferring to a sealed bag or container.

READY MIXED BAGS

Freeze ready-mixed bags of vegetables to use, cut into similar-sized pieces. (Ex. root vegetable medley or stir fry medley).

TIP: Use a french fry cutter for quick + easy uniform chopping of your root vegetables or potatoes for freezing (pictured).

LABEL IT

Be sure to label bags/containers with the date frozen, so you can keep track of the items in your freezer. It is recommended to eat frozen food within 8-12 months. Though they can last longer than this, they will begin to deteriorate in quality and flavour.

KEEP A RECORD

Consider keeping a record of how much food you are preserving each year to evaluate whether you're putting away too much, not enough, or exactly how much you need.

CANNING YOUR VEGETABLES

Canning is a convenient way to preserve your vegetables right on the pantry shelf, where they can last for years. It also offers many creative options to stock your pantry with vegetables (such as salsas, relishes, savoury jams, chutneys, sauces, and more) and is easier than you might imagine.

There are two methods for canning:

WATER BATH CANNING + PRESSURE CANNING

Both methods involve preparing food and placing it in sealed jars, which are then heated properly to a specified temperature to prevent harmful bacteria from growing on the food.

The benefit of water bath canning is that it's simpler and doesn't require specialized equipment (you can do it with just a large pot). However, it is only safe for items with high enough amounts of sugar or acidity. Pressure canning, on the other hand, can be used to preserve all kinds of items, including plain vegetables, but it requires a specialized kitchen appliance (pressure canner). See individual vegetable pages for specific canning instructions.

Always follow the proper procedures to prevent foodborne illnesses when doing home canning.

WATER BATH CANNING

This method can be used to preserve any foods containing high enough amounts of acidity or sugar, such as fruits, salsas, jams, relishes, and tomatoes.

Water bath canning involves boiling your filled, sealed jars in water for the specified amount of time stated in your recipe. This method doesn't require any special equipment (you can use a large stockpot with a folded tea towel in the bottom if you don't have a water bath canner). However there are some helpful canning utensils you'll likely want to purchase. We recommend a canning funnel and jar lifter to make things easier. Just be sure to follow recipe guidelines for the appropriate canning time to ensure the safety of your home canned goods. Find yourself a recipe and give it a whirl.

PRESSURE CANNING

Pressure canning requires a specialized piece of equipment (pressure canner) that looks like a heavy-duty pot with a locking lid and a pressure gauge, used to monitor the pressure inside the canner during processing.

You must use this method when canning plain vegetables. The boiling water bath method is not sufficient to properly preserve low-acid foods like vegetables, and deadly foodborne illnesses can occur. Pressure canning, on the other hand, can process food at higher temperatures, well above boiling, to effectively prevent spoilage and ensure food safety. Pressure canning can be used with all kinds of preserves, but it is the only safe way to can plain vegetables. You can do it with raw vegetables (raw pack method), boiled vegetables (hot pack method), and freshly prepared items like soups, stews, sauces, or broths that do not contain thickeners, dairy, or starches (these things can be added and cooked in before serving if desired).

It is unsafe to pressure can puréed, mashed, or shredded vegetables as the heat cannot fully penetrate such densely packed food enough to prevent risk.

Supplies needed for canning vegetables:

Canning jars + lids (use new lids each year to ensure a tight seal)

Large pot or **water bath canner** (simply use a large pot with a folded tea towel in the bottom if you don't have a water bath canner) or **pressure canner**

Jar lifter

Canning funnel

STEP-BY-STEP
WATER BATH CANNING
Salsas, jams, pickles, relishes, and tomatoes

1. Wash canning jars and lids in hot, soapy water. Rinse. (There is no need to sterilize jars when processing them over 10 minutes.) Keep lids in hot (not boiling) water until ready to use.

2. **Follow a recipe for making the salsa, jam, pickles, or relish.** For canning tomatoes, prepare your tomatoes by peeling (pg 274) and chopping them to desired size. Place in pot, bring to boil. Boil for 5 minutes, stirring occasionally.

3. **Fill jars with hot item using a canning funnel, leaving 1/2" headspace (the space between the surface of the food and the underside of the lid).** With canned tomatoes, it is recommended to add bottled lemon juice (1 tbsp per pint jar, 2 tbsp per quart jar) to ensure proper acidity.

6. Wipe rims of the jars with a clean, damp towel to ensure a proper seal. Screw on lids.

7. Load the jars into a canner (or large stockpot with a folded teatowel in the bottom). Fill the pot with water, ensuring it covers the jars by at least 1-2 inches.

8. Bring the water to a boil. Once boiling, start the timer for the recommended processing time. (NOTE: process times increase with your altitude. Above 1000ft, add 5 minutes more; above 3000ft, add 10 minutes more)
Recommended processing time for canning diced or crushed tomatoes is 45 minutes (increase for higher altitudes).

9. After processing, turn off the heat. Carefully remove hot jars with a jar lifter and place them on a clean, dry towel or cooling rack. Let the jars cool completely. You should hear the lids "pop" as they seal.

10. Check the seals after 24 hours (press the center of the jar lid with your finger; it should not move or give when pressed). If a jar does not seal, refrigerate or reprocess it.

STEP-BY-STEP
PRESSURE CANNING VEGETABLES

1. Wash canning jars and lids in hot, soapy water. Rinse. (There is no need to sterilize jars when processing them over 10 minutes.) Keep lids in hot (not boiling) water until ready to use.

2. Wash, peel, and prepare your vegetables, cutting them to desired size. At this point, you can keep them raw or boil them partially first, depending on your preference (keep in mind they will cook some during canning).

3. Pack the jars with prepared vegetables, leaving 1" headspace (the space between the surface of the food and the underside of the lid).

4. If desired, add salt to each jar for flavour (up to 1 tsp salt per quart jar). Adjust to your tastes or omit it altogether. (It is not a safety requirement to add any salt when pressure canning vegetables.)

5. Fill packed jars with water (leaving 1" headspace), removing any air bubbles with a bubble remover tool, chopstick, or butter knife.

6. Wipe rims of the jars with a clean, damp towel to ensure a proper seal. Screw on lids.

7. Load jars into the pressure canner. Add 2 to 3 inches of water in the bottom and follow the manufacturer's instructions for use (locking, venting, and pressurizing the canner).

8. Once the canner reaches the desired pressure, start a timer. Process the jars for the recommended time for that item. (See vegetable pages for individual processing times.)

9. After processing, turn off the heat and let the canner depressurize naturally, following the manufacturer's instructions. Do not force-cool or open the canner until it has depressurized completely.

10. Use a jar lifter to carefully remove hot jars from the canner. Place them on a clean, dry towel or cooling rack. Let the jars cool completely. You should hear the lids "pop" as they seal.

11. Check the seals after 24 hours (press the center of the jar lid with your finger; it should not move or give when pressed). If a jar did not seal, refrigerate or reprocess it.

Use your vegetable scraps to make soup broths.
Save and freeze those ends and peels along the way for added flavour and nutrition to your broths.

MAKES 10 QUART JARS

VEGETABLE BROTH

We use a lot of vegetable broth in our house— not just in soups, but in our stews, rice, risottos, and sauces too. It's something I always like to have on hand. I usually pressure can a big batch in the fall, and freeze some smaller batches during the year once that runs out. This recipe is completely versatile and can be adapted to use whatever veggie extras you have lying about. Add in leftover bones to make this a nourishing bone broth.

2 tbsp oil
1 large onion with skins, loosely chopped
4 cloves garlic, chopped
2 large carrots with skins, chopped
2 stalks celery and leaves, loosely chopped
1 tbsp salt (plus more to taste)

40 cups water (or simply fill the stockpot)
4 rough cups spare vegetables or pieces (peels, ends, greens), loosely chopped
3 bay leaves
2 tbsp tomato paste
Fresh ground black pepper

In a large stock pot, add oil. Over medium heat, sauté onions, garlic, carrots, and celery. Add salt and stir to coat. Continue to cook, stirring frequently, until somewhat softened.

Add water and spare vegetables. Stir in the remaining ingredients. Cover with a lid, increase heat and bring to a boil. Reduce heat to simmer and allow to cook for 45-60 minutes. Taste and adjust the flavour to your liking. Remove from heat. Strain liquid into another pot for use or preserve through one of the following:

FREEZING: Allow to cool completely. Transfer to freezer containers (leave 1" headspace).
CANNING: While still hot, strain portions at a time into a pitcher for pouring directly into jars (leaving 1" headspace). Follow pressure canning directions on pg 57 from step 6 onwards.

DEHYDRATING YOUR VEGETABLES

Dehydrating is a great way to extend the shelf life of your vegetables while creating a concentrated source of flavour and nutrition. Dehydrated food retains its original nutritional value and simply loses its water content. It takes little room to store, makes for low-prep cooking later on, and lasts up to 12 months if stored properly.

There are three methods for dehydrating:

DEHYDRATOR + OVEN + SUN DRYING

All three methods involve spreading sliced produce in a single layer on trays or baking sheets and allowing them to sit for many hours, with heat and air circulating around them to evaporate the moisture.

A food dehydrator is a great investment if you plan to dry foods regularly. If not, an oven on a low setting or time in the hot sun will do the trick. Sun drying takes the longest (days to weeks), while the other two methods require anywhere from 2-12 hours to dehydrate your produce, depending on the type of vegetable and the thickness of the pieces. Whichever your chosen method, I recommend purchasing a mandolin slicer to help you cut thin, uniform slices—it's a dehydration time saver.

Dehydrating offers a practical way to preserve and enjoy the nutritional benefits and concentrated flavours of your fresh produce all year long. Dehydrated vegetables are especially great if you're an outdoor enthusiast looking for lightweight and portable food options, want long-term food storage, or emergency preparedness.

FOOD DEHYDRATOR

A food dehydrator is an electric appliance designed specifically for drying foods. It has stackable trays or shelves for arranging sliced produce and a fan that circulates warm air to remove moisture. The benefit of using a dehydrator is its precise temperature control and consistent air circulation, giving you consistent results. It requires electricity and will run for hours on end, but it is more energy efficient than using the oven if you plan on dehydrating frequently or in large batches.

OVEN DRYING

This method involves placing vegetables on parchment-lined baking sheets and dehydrating them in a conventional oven at the lowest possible temperature (usually around 140-160°F or 60-70°C). Low and slow is the key to avoiding cooking or baking the vegetable with the oven method. If your oven has a convection setting, use it to improve air circulation. Prop the oven door open slightly using a wooden spoon to allow moisture to escape. Depending on your oven, you may need to rotate the trays periodically to ensure even drying.

Oven dehydration takes less time than using a food dehydrator but can be less energy efficient and may not produce as even results.

SUN DRYING

Sun drying is the traditional method of dehydrating vegetables. It involves placing thinly sliced vegetables on screens or trays in direct sunlight. The heat from the sun evaporates the moisture over time. This method requires hot, dry weather and can take several days. Choose a location with ample sunlight exposure throughout the day, and cover the trays at night to protect them from dew or moisture.

The advantage of sun drying is that it's a natural, low-cost method. The disadvantages are that it relies on weather conditions and requires much longer drying times. Sun drying is not recommended in areas with high humidity, as the risk of spoilage increases.

If using this method, consider finishing the drying process indoors using a dehydrator or oven to enhance safety and prevent the growth of harmful microorganisms- especially if outdoor conditions are not optimal for sun drying.

HANG DRYING GREENS + HERBS

Hang drying is the traditional method for preserving herbs or leafy greens with low moisture content (like kale or spinach).

Tie small bunches of greens together at the stems using a string or twine. Hang bunches upside down from a hook or line in a dry area with good air circulation. Choose a location away from direct sunlight to prevent loss of colour and flavour. Cover with cheesecloth if you are concerned about dust or insects. Check on them regularly. Hang drying takes 1-2 weeks.

Once the greens are thoroughly dried and crisp, remove the leaves from the stems and store them in mason jars or airtight containers. (Greens and herbs can also be dehydrated using an oven or dehydrator.)

FREEZE DRYING is another method for dehydrating vegetables. It is excellent at preserving vegetable quality but requires expensive, specialized equipment that is not as common or accessible for home use.

STEP-BY-STEP FOR DEHYDRATING

1. Wash, peel, and slice vegetables uniformly to ensure even drying. Slice them thinly. I recommend using a mandolin slicer. Thicker pieces take much longer to dehydrate.

2. Blanching (optional). Some vegetables benefit from blanching (page 48) before dehydration to preserve colour and texture and extend shelf life. (See individual vegetable pages for specific dehydrating instructions.) Pat dry with a paper towel or cloth.

3. Arrange the prepared vegetables on dehydrator trays, baking sheets, or other drying surfaces.

4. Follow specific instructions and drying times for your chosen dehydration method. Vegetables can scorch easily toward the end of drying, so monitor them more closely towards the end.

5. Vegetables are adequately dehydrated when brittle and no longer moist. Check multiple pieces for consistency.

6. Allow your dehydrated vegetables to cool before storing them in airtight containers or turning them into powders. (Grind with a food processor, mortar and pestle, spice grinder, or coffee grinder to make powder.) Store in a pantry or cupboard away from moisture and direct sunlight.

Dehydrating Tips

REHYDRATING

Dehydrated vegetables can be rehydrated by soaking them in hot water or adding them directly to your cooking with recipes that contain a fair amount of liquid, such as soups, stews, casseroles, or sauces.

NOTE: They will absorb moisture as they rehydrate, thickening the soup or stew. Be sure to include enough liquid (or rehydrate first).

STORING

Dried vegetables must be sealed in airtight containers like mason jars, freezer bags, or with a vacuum sealer and stored in a pantry or cupboard away from moisture and direct sunlight. They last up to 12 months if stored properly.

INTENSIFIED FLAVOUR

Dehydrating concentrates the natural flavours of vegetables, making them a flavour-boosting addition to various dishes. Since dehydrated items can be more potent than fresh, start by adding smaller amounts to recipes and adjust to your taste.

POWDERS

Grind dehydrated vegetables into powders using a food processor, mortar and pestle, spice grinder, or coffee grinder. Powders add extra flavour and nutrition to recipes.

Powders can also be used as a natural food colouring in things like homemade pasta dough, salad dressings, frostings, and desserts. (Ex. spinach or kale for green, beet for pink, carrot or sweet potato for orange). Always start with a small amount and gradually adjust based on your taste preferences.

CUSTOM TRAIL MIX

You can enjoy your dehydrated vegetables on their own as a crunchy snack or combine them with nuts and seeds to create a custom trail mix.

INSTANT SOUP MIX

Create your own homemade instant soup mix by combining dehydrated vegetables, noodles, and seasonings. Add boiling water to make a quick and convenient soup.

MAKES 1/4 CUP

DEHYDRATED VEGETABLE SEASONING MIX

This is a delicious way to use up those extra veggie bits for all kinds of flavour down the line. I use this seasoning for a dip mix, in salad dressing, dry rubs or marinades, to make a flavourful risotto, and to add seasoning to roasted potatoes or vegetables. With high flavour intensity, a little powder goes a long way (only a teaspoon or tablespoon at a time is needed) and lasts up to a year. This recipe is versatile; you can go beyond what I have used here. Add other dried vegetables or herbs to your liking. Consider it your creative starting point.

1 med onion, sliced thinly (or fresh green tops)
2 ribs celery, thinly sliced (or celery leaves)
1 head garlic, cloves peeled and sliced thinly (or garlic scapes)

Slice vegetables thinly; thicker pieces take much longer to dehydrate.
You can dehydrate them using a dehydrator (feel free to multiply for a larger batch) or follow the oven-drying method below.

Oven drying method:
Arrange sliced vegetables in a single layer on a large parchment-lined baking sheet. If your oven has a convection option that works at a low temperature (between 140-170°F), you can double or triple this recipe to make multiple baking sheets simultaneously. If not, stick to one large baking sheet.

As a pre-treatment, you can bake the vegetable slices at 350° for 5 minutes, then turn down the oven to the lowest possible temperature (usually around 140-170°F). Use the convection setting or oven fan if possible to keep air circulating (if your oven doesn't have this option, that's okay). Prop the oven door open a crack with a wooden spoon or utensil to allow moisture to escape during the process. Dehydrate this way for 3-5 hours or until vegetables are brittle and no longer moist. Check multiple pieces for consistency. (Garlic slices or leaves may dry faster than items with higher moisture content; if done early, transfer them to a plate and allow them to cool.)

(Seasoning Mix continued)

Once dehydrated:
Always allow dehydrated vegetables to cool before turning them into powders or storing them. I like to leave them in an open container on the kitchen counter overnight to ensure they are as dry as possible before grinding them into powder the next day.

Grind dehydrated vegetables with a food processor, mortar and pestle, spice grinder, or coffee grinder to make powder. Place powder in a sealed jar or container. Store in the pantry or cupboard away from moisture and direct sunlight. Lasts up to a year.

FAVOURITE WAYS TO USE

- Veggie Dip -
1 tbsp seasoning, 2/3 cup sour cream, 1/3 cup mayonnaise
Store in refrigerator. Allow flavours to meld. Serve with fresh veggies for dipping.
(Makes 1 cup)

- Dry rub -
2 tsp seasoning mix, 1 tsp paprika, 1 tsp salt, 1 tsp chili powder, 1 tbsp brown sugar
Combine and rub over meat to coat before cooking.
(Makes 2 1/2 tbsp)

- Wet Rub -
2 tsp seasoning mix, 1 tsp paprika, 1 tsp salt, 1 tsp oregano, 3 tbsp olive oil
Combine to form a paste. Smear over meat, coating well. Refrigerate in a sealed bag or container for 30 minutes to overnight.
(Makes 1/4 cup)

- Favourite Ranch Dressing -
1 tsp seasoning mix, ½ tsp dried parsley, ½ tsp dried dill, fresh ground pepper, ½ cup mayonnaise, ¼ cup milk, and juice of half a lemon
Combine in small jar or container. Store in refrigerator.
(Makes 1 cup)

FERMENTING YOUR VEGETABLES

Fermenting foods is an ancient form of preservation that goes back thousands of years. It's a combination of science and art that extends the shelf life of your fresh vegetables, gives them a tangy flavour, and creates probiotic-rich foods that provide numerous health benefits.

The process of fermenting produce (known as Lacto-Fermentation) is simpler than you think and only requires a jar, some salt, and the vegetables you choose. It's a natural process in which prepared vegetables sit in a jar in your cupboard or pantry shelf for several weeks. During this time, the sugars in the vegetables turn into lactic acid, which acts as a natural preservative, creating probiotic activity and developing that signature sour or tangy taste.

Once the vegetables have fermented to your desired taste and acidity, they are moved to the refrigerator to slow the fermentation process. Fermented vegetables should be stored in your refrigerator, lasting several months to a year.

There are many ways to ferment your fresh produce and reap the incredible health benefits, including fermented pickles, fermented salsas, fermented shredded veggies for sandwiches and salads, or just a plain jar of some fermented vegetables for snacking. Two of the most commonly known fermented foods would be sauerkraut (cabbage) and kimchi (cabbage, mixed vegetables, and spices), both made using those crunchy garden vegetables.

FERMENTING

Lacto-fermentation (the method used in fermenting vegetables) involves submerging chopped or shredded vegetables in a salt brine (adding in herbs, spices, honey, or vinegar for additional flavour if desired) and waiting (typically 1-4 weeks) until they reach the desired taste.

You can ferment raw, cooked, or blanched vegetables. With fermentation, the probiotic content (the microorganisms that benefit your gut health) is established early on, while the flavours continue to develop over time. Experimenting with different fermentation times allows you to find the blend of flavours and textures you enjoy most. Some people prefer a shorter fermentation for a milder taste and crunchier vegetable, while others like to let it ferment longer for a more robust flavour and softer vegetable. Start tasting your fermenting vegetables after the first week, and continue to taste periodically until you achieve your desired flavour and texture.

Once the vegetables reach your desired level of fermentation, seal them in an airtight container and move them to the refrigerator to slow down the process. Fermentation will continue but at a much slower rate. Fermented vegetables can be stored in the refrigerator (in a sealed jar or airtight container) for several months to a year, depending on the conditions. Regularly check the appearance and aroma of your fermented vegetables and use your judgment to determine if they are still good for consumption.

SALT is the essential ingredient in all vegetable fermentations
There are two methods for adding salt in lacto-fermentation:

DRY SALTING- Use if vegetables are shredded, finely chopped, or have high enough water content (ex. sauerkraut, kimchi, shredded vegetables, or fermented salsa). Dry salting produces superior flavour (the water in brine dilutes flavour).

BRINE- Salt plus water. Used when vegetables are whole or chunky or will not produce enough liquid on their own to be covered (e.g., fermented pickles, carrot sticks, beans).

For fermentation to occur, it is essential to keep the vegetables submerged in liquid. Salt draws the liquid out of the vegetables (as well as slowing their softening and giving them flavour). Some vegetables have less water content and will not produce enough liquid on their own to be submerged; this is when adding brine is needed.

Supplies needed for fermenting vegetables:

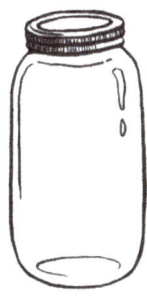

Non-iodized salt (preferably sea salt or kosher salt)
Wide-mouth glass jar (or ceramic crock, or food-grade plastic container)
Weight to keep the vegetables submerged in brine (e.g., fermentation weight, smaller jar, trimmed cabbage leaf, a clean rock)
Lid or cloth secured with rubber band, for covering the jar
Kitchen scale for calculating salt amount
Water (non-chlorinated), for brine method only

FERMENTING FOOD IS BOTH A SCIENCE AND AN ART
It takes experimentation to find the flavour and texture that you like best.

Ferments are best enjoyed in their natural state. Cooking fermented vegetables kills the beneficial bacteria that are so good for your gut health.

FERMENT YOUR VEGETABLES

1. Wash and slice (or shred) vegetables into the desired size. You can add herbs, spices, additional vegetables such as garlic or onions, honey, or vinegar for added flavour.

2. Add salt. The amount of salt needed is measured in percentage. You want to stick between 2% and 5% of the weight or volume of your ingredients. (2% is the minimum percentage of salt needed for fermentation to work properly and be safe. Anything higher than 5%, and you risk stopping the fermentation.) You can experiment depending on your tastes. Less salt will mean faster fermentation, and more salt means a crunchier texture and greater mold resistance.

The general recommendation is a salt ratio of 2%. Here's how to calculate your amount:

FOR DRY SALTING,
Weigh your prepared ingredients in grams with a kitchen scale (be sure to subtract the weight of the bowl holding them first). Then multiply that number by 0.02 (2%) to give you the amount of salt needed to add. For example,

$$250g \text{ prepared vegetables} \times 0.02 \text{ (2\%)} = 5g \text{ salt}$$

Using your hands, massage the salt into the vegetables, then leave them to soak for 15 minutes. Pack them tightly down in a jar, pressing hard to release juices. If needed, supplement with additional salt water to ensure vegetables are fully covered. Do not fill past the neck of the jar to allow for bubbling.

FOR BRINE,
Check the volume of the jar you plan to fill. Multiply that number by 0.02 (2%) to give you the amount of salt needed to add. For example,

$$500mL \text{ jar} \times 0.02 \text{ (2\%)} = 10g \text{ salt}$$

Fill your jar with prepared vegetables. Add in the salt. Pour in enough water to cover the vegetables completely. Do not fill past the neck of the jar, allowing headspace for bubbling.

3. Add a weight or trimmed cabbage leaf to keep vegetables submerged. Cover with a lid or a cloth secured with rubber band. If using a lid, burp it once a day allowing gases to escape. Place in a dark, room-temperature location (kitchen cupboard or pantry shelf is perfect). Fermentation can take anywhere from a few days to several weeks.

4. Periodically check the vegetables, tasting them to monitor their flavour and acidity. Once your desired level of tanginess is reached, the fermentation can be considered complete. Store them in the refrigerator in a sealed jar or airtight container, lasting several months to a year. Check regularly.

PICKLING YOUR VEGETABLES

Most vegetables will stand up well to pickling and make delightful snacks, zingy toppers on sandwiches or tacos, or tasty additions to salads and sides, giving an extra flavour punch to your meals throughout the year. Pickling is also a great way to extend the life of vegetables you won't have time to enjoy fresh.

There are three methods for pickling:

CLASSIC PICKLE + QUICK PICKLE + SLOW PICKLE

Both the classic and quick pickling methods are made by packing vegetable pieces into a jar and pouring a heated vinegar brine (mixture of salt, vinegar, water, and sometimes sugar) over it. Quick pickles are quick and easy to make, ready within hours, and have a shorter shelf life (they must be kept in the refrigerator and eaten within a month of making them). Classic pickles are a little more time-intensive (involving the canning process) but are flavour-rich and can be stored in a cupboard or pantry for years until use.

Slow pickles, on the other hand, are made through the fermentation process in a saltwater brine. This method is slower and more gradual, taking weeks to months and developing complex flavours and probiotic benefits. Slow pickles get their tanginess from fermentation rather than from vinegar.

You can make your pickle batches as small or large as you like, from one jar to dozens at a time. (See individual veggie pages for pickling inspiration.) Pickling dates back to medieval times, another way our ancestors preserved food for use throughout the year before refrigeration was possible.

CLASSIC PICKLING

This method is used to preserve many of the vegetables we love, adding vibrancy, zest, and all kinds of unique flavouring options to enjoy through the off-season. A handful of vegetables don't stand up well to classic pickling (see vegetable pages for specific pickling directions), but the majority will surprise you with their versatility!

The process involves preparing and stuffing your vegetables into jars (perhaps adding garlic, spices or herbs), then pouring your heated vinegar brine over top. After securing the lids, you will process the jars by immersing them in boiling water for a designated amount of time (using the water bath canning method), typically between 10-30 minutes, then removing them from the water bath and allowing them to cool until the lids "pop" indicating they have sealed. This heat treatment is necessary to store your pickles at room temperature as it destroys the micro-organisms that cause spoilage.

Once sealed, pickles can last 1-2 years on a pantry shelf. After opening, they must be kept in the refrigerator and eaten within a month. Always follow recipe guidelines for appropriate canning time to ensure the safety of your home-canned goods.

QUICK PICKLING

Also known as refrigerator pickles, this method is quick and easy, super flavourful, and a fun way to stretch a little more life out of a veggie that has been hanging out too long in your refrigerator. The best part is that they are ready to eat within hours. These pickles are typically made in smaller quantities—a jar at a time—since they don't last as long.

All that's needed is your chopped or sliced vegetable (or veggie medley) placed in a jar or bowl. Pour a heated vinegar brine over top and allow it to sit and absorb the flavours for a couple of hours or overnight, transferring to the refrigerator once cooled. Quick pickles are best enjoyed within a few weeks to a month. They are not meant for long-term shelf storage like traditional canned pickles.

SLOW PICKLING

This method of pickling involves fermentation in a saltwater brine to create tanginess rather than marinating in a vinegar brine. It is the traditional way to pickle, relying on natural processes. For this method, head to pg 74.

Supplies needed for pickling vegetables:

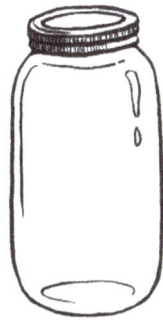

Vinegar (white, apple cider, or pickling vinegar; at least 5% acidity)
Water
Salt (pickling salt or kosher salt)
Flavour additions (optional) (ex. spices, herbs, sugar, garlic)

Classic pickling also requires:

Canning jars + lids (use new lids each year to ensure a tight seal)
Large pot or **water bath canner** (simply use a large pot with a folded tea towel in the bottom if you don't have a water bath canner)
Jar lifter
Canning funnel (optional)

MAKES 5 PINT JARS

CLASSIC PICKLED

This is my favourite go-to recipe for canning pickled veggies on the farm. We enjoy eating them straight out of the jar and using them as flavourful toppers on all kinds of meals. The best part is that they last all year round!

8 -10 cups whole, chopped, or sliced vegetable/s of choice
2 1/2 cup white vinegar (5% acidity or higher)
2 1/2 cup water
1/4 cup pickling salt or kosher salt
2 tbsp sugar
Aromatics or spices (optional), pg 82

Wash canning jars and lids in hot, soapy water. Rinse. There is no need to sterilize jars when you will be processing over 10 minutes. Keep lids in hot (not boiling) water until ready to use.

Make your brine. Combine vinegar, water, salt, and sugar in a saucepan. Bring to a boil, turn down the heat, cover and simmer until ready to use.

Pack prepared vegetables in jars, adding in any aromatics or spices. Using a canning funnel, pour hot brine over top, completely covering the vegetables (allowing 1/2" headspace at the top). Wipe rims of the jars with a clean, damp towel to ensure a proper seal. Screw on lids.

Load the jars into a canner (or large stockpot with a folded tea towel in the bottom). Fill the pot with water, covering the jars by at least 1 inch.

Bring the water to a boil. Boil for the recommended processing time (see individual vegetable pages), adjusting for altitude (see note). After processing, turn off the heat. Carefully remove hot jars with a jar lifter and place them on a clean, dry towel or cooling rack. Let the jars cool completely. You should hear the lids "pop" as they seal.

Check the seals after 24 hours (press the center of the jar lid with your finger; it should not move or give when pressed). If a jar did not seal, refrigerate or reprocess it. For best flavour, wait at least 4-6 weeks before enjoying. Canned pickles last 1-2 years on the pantry shelf. Store pickles in the refrigerator once opened, and eat within 4 weeks.

NOTE: Processing times increase with your altitude. Above 1000ft add 5 minutes more; above 3000ft add 10 minutes more.

MAKES 2 PINT JARS (1 QUART JAR)

QUICK PICKLED

Quick pickling couldn't be easier and adds so much fun and vibrancy to a dish. I love that I can whip these up on a whim with whatever I have on hand. I often use this recipe plain (with no aromatics or spices added), allowing just the vegetable to shine, but feel free to play and add unique flavours to your liking.

4 cups chopped or sliced vegetable/s of choice
1 cup white vinegar (or vinegar of choice)
1 cup water
1 tbsp pickling salt or kosher salt
1-2 tbsp sugar
Aromatics or spices (optional), pg 82

Place prepared vegetables in a jar/s or glass bowl, adding any aromatics or spices.

In a saucepan, combine vinegar, water, salt, and sugar. Bring to a boil.

Pour over vegetables, making sure to submerge them completely. Allow to cool before transferring to the refrigerator. Chill for a few hours or overnight before enjoying. The longer they sit, the more flavour they will absorb. Lasts 4 weeks in an airtight jar or container.

Store in refrigerator.

AROMATICS + SPICES

Add your own selection of these to your jar of pickles
for extra flavour and depth.

Peeled garlic clove, peeled ginger, sprig of dill or dill seeds, sprig of thyme, fennel frond or seeds, peppercorns, mustard seeds, coriander seeds, celery seeds, caraway seeds, chili powder, paprika, oregano, turmeric, whole cloves, allspice, star anise, nutmeg, cinnamon, cardamom, bay leaf
For spicy pickles: add a pinch of red pepper flakes or cayenne pepper

FAVOURITE FLAVOUR COMBOS
(to each jar add):

- Dill pickled -
Peeled garlic clove, sprig of fresh dill

- Ginger pickled -
1-2 slices fresh ginger (or 1/4 tsp ground ginger),
1 tsp honey, pinch of red pepper flakes

- Italian Pickled -
Peeled garlic clove, 1/4 tsp celery seed,
1/4 tsp fennel seed or frond, 1/2 tsp oregano,
1 bay leaf

- Citrus Pickled -
1 tsp honey, juice of half a lemon/lime/orange

- Spicy Cinnamon -
Peeled garlic clove, 1/4 tsp cinnamon, bay leaf, pinch red pepper flakes

- Taco Spiced -
Peeled garlic clove, 1/2 tsp chili powder, 1/2 tsp paprika,
1/4 tsp each cumin, onion powder,
oregano, pinch of cayenne pepper

- Curry Pickled -
1/2 tsp curry powder, 1/4 tsp each turmeric +
mustard seeds, pinch of red pepper flakes

Don't discard the pickling liquid after eating those tasty pickles. Repurpose it for salad dressings, marinades, or to quick pickle other vegetables.

MAKES 2/3 CUP

TANGY PICKLING LIQUID SALAD DRESSING

Another flavourful way to use what you've got to further enjoy all those vegetables. Drizzle this over a fresh garden salad, veggie grain bowl, or warm roasted vegetable medley.

1/3 cup pickling liquid
1/3 cup olive oil
1 tbsp dijon mustard
1 tsp honey
Pepper to taste

Add all ingredients to a small container or pint-sized mason jar. Screw on lid, and shake to combine. Stores in refrigerator up to one week.

Before you dive into the vegetable pages...

There are many ways vegetables can be categorized (such as botanical classification, plant family, culinary use, and more). For this book I have grouped them based on the part of the plant that is eaten.

ROOTS

Vegetables // that grow underground

BEETS

Robust root vegetable with sweet, earthy flavour.

← Leaves are edible. A wonderful substitute for spinach or swiss chard in recipes, they are delicious braised, sautéed, and suitable for eating raw in sandwiches or salads.

← Stems are nutritious too, though bitter and often discarded. You can pickle or sauté them with the greens.

← Root is delicious boiled, sautéed, chopped, roasted, served over salads, puréed into sauces, in baking, or added to smoothies. Enjoy peeled or unpeeled. Pairs well with citrus.

FRESH STORAGE	Remove leafy stems from beets (they draw moisture away from the root), leaving a small portion of stems attached. Store leaves and roots separately in sealed bags or containers in the refrigerator. Wash leaves when ready to use. Leaves last up to 2 weeks, roots last for months.
QUIRKS	Once peeled or chopped, beets will bleed on other veggies, causing them to take on their rich red colour. Because of this, you may wish to cook them separately from other items.
PRESERVATION	Freeze, pressure can, dehydrate, ferment, or pickle. (See next page for more) Beet tops can also be preserved through freezing, dehydrating, and turning into powder for added nutrition in recipes, or made into pesto (pg 39) and frozen. Follow methods for swiss chard greens (pg 208).

Batch Prep Beets

The simplest way to ready your beets for use or preservation

Remove leafy tops, leave a small portion of stems on (don't slice the actual beet skin, or juices will bleed out), and leave the skin and root on. Roast or boil whole until tender.

ROAST WHOLE: Preheat your oven to 400°F (200°C). Rub beets in olive oil (coat well), wrap individually in aluminum foil, and roast for about 45-60 minutes until tender when pierced with a fork.

BOIL WHOLE: Place whole beets in a pot of water. Cover, bring to a boil. Boil until fork tender (30-45 minutes, depending on size), remove from heat and allow to cool. (If needed, run under cold water to speed up the cooling process until cool enough to handle.)

Once cooled, slice off the tops and bottoms. The skins will slip right off to reveal brightly cooked beets ready for use. Chop, slice, or purée as needed. Store in the refrigerator (up to 6 days) for use in salads, sides, smoothies, baking, or favourite beet recipes all week. Or freeze, can, or pickle to use throughout the year.

BAKING WITH BEETS
adds a natural sweetness and moisture to your baking, resulting in a fudgy, delicious treat.

Use cooked beet purée (pg 41) or grated beets in baking recipes. The naturally brilliant colour of red beets gives an appealing 'red velvet' tinge to cakes, brownies, and cupcakes without any artificial colouring.

You can also use beet juice or dehydrated beet powder (pg 63) as a natural pink food colouring for frosting or other recipes.

FREEZING YOUR BEETS

You can freeze your beets raw, blanched, or cooked (pg 48). All three work great. Freeze them sliced, grated, puréed, or chopped, depending on your purpose. I recommend **peeling them first** to improve texture and flavour. (Freeze purées in pre-portioned amounts (such as 1 cup or 2 cups) based on what you plan to use it in. pg 41)

TO USE: Can cook directly from frozen.
Turn chopped or sliced beets into borscht, roasted beets, beet salad, beet mash, beet juice, or add them to smoothies. Grated beets can be made into beet fritters, beet slaw, or beet risotto. Puréed beets can be used in baking (beet brownies, cake, muffins), made into beet hummus, beet dip, or beet burgers.

CANNING YOUR BEETS

You can preserve beets through **pressure canning** for use in soups (such as borscht), salads, in your favourite beet recipes, or as a side. Cook and peel them first (pg 90), then can them whole, cubed, or sliced. Pressure canning steps, pg 57
Processing time: 30 min (pints) 35 min (quarts)

DEHYDRATING YOUR BEETS

Beets take around 8-12 hours to dehydrate, depending on the thickness of the slices and moisture content. Batch boil beets for 20 minutes first to easily remove skin (pg 94) and prep for drying. Dehydrating steps, pg 63

TO USE: Enjoy dehydrated beet chips as a crunchy snack. Grind them into a powder as a colour addition for dips (beet hummus or tzatziki), homemade pasta (pink ravioli), smoothies, baking (red velvet cake or pink pancakes) or as a garnish. Dehydrated beets can also be rehydrated and added to soups, risottos, pastas, or warm salads.

FERMENTING YOUR BEETS

Fermenting beets creates a probiotic-rich, tangy condiment to use in salads, sandwiches, mixed into dips and sauces, or as a side dish. Remove beet skins with a vegetable peeler, shred, small dice, or slice. Or cook and peel them first (pg 94) for a softer fermented product. Fermenting steps, pg 74

TO USE: Add fermented beets to salads, wraps, or sandwiches for a burst of flavour and probiotics. Blend fermented beets with other ingredients like (onions, mustard, and vinegar) to create a tasty beet relish for hot dogs or sandwiches. Purée fermented beets and mix them into sauces, salad dressings, hummus, or vinaigrettes for added depth, colour and nutrition. Or serve fermented beets as a tangy side dish alongside roasted or grilled meats and vegetables.

PICKLING YOUR BEETS

Beets can be plain pickled or flavoured in any number of sweet or savoury pickle variations (such as honey + ginger pickled, curry pickled, dill pickled, spicy pickled) to enjoy throughout the year. Remove skins with a vegetable peeler and slice thinly to pickle raw (for crunch). Or cook first, then peel beets (pg 94). Slice, cube, or cut into wedges. Pickling steps, pg 80 or 81   **Processing time (water bath canning):30 min**

TO USE: Pickled beets are a delicious pantry treat enjoyed straight from the jar, served alongside charcuterie or cheese boards, on burgers, sandwiches, or hot dogs, or to add a delicious zing to salads.

CARROTS
—

Crunchy, tapered root vegetable with sweet, earthy taste.

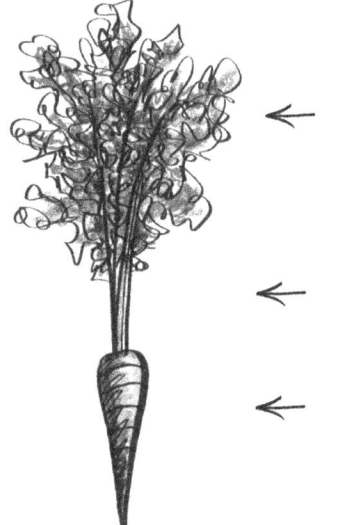

← Leafy carrot tops are edible and herbaceous, particularly in early summer when they are young and tender. Tear feathery leaves from the bitter stalk and try substituting them for fresh herbs in recipes, sautéing alongside vegetables, adding to smoothies, or making carrot top pesto (pg 39).

← Stems are bitter and woody and should be discarded.

← Root is delicious raw as a snack, shredded in salads, wraps, or coleslaws. Try it roasted, steamed, sautéed with spices, tossed with a dollop of butter and fresh herbs, or added to soups, stews, and stir-fries. Enjoy it peeled or unpeeled.

FRESH STORAGE Remove leafy tops (they draw moisture away from the carrot) and stringy root. Store tops and carrots separately in sealed bags or containers in the refrigerator. Tops last a week, carrots last for months.

PRESERVATION Freeze, pressure can, dehydrate, ferment, or pickle.
(See next page for more)

Carrot tops can be preserved through freezing, dehydrating and turned into powder for added nutrition in recipes or made into pesto and frozen (pg 39).

FREEZING YOUR CARROTS

You can freeze carrots raw, blanched, or cooked (pg 48).
Freeze them chopped, grated, or puréed, depending on your purpose. **Freeze purée in pre-portioned amounts** (such as 1 cup or 2 cups) based on what you plan to use it for.

TO USE: Can cook directly from frozen.
Add your chopped frozen carrots directly to cooking such as soups, stews, casseroles, stir fries, or plain roasted. Add them to smoothies or make carrot juice. Grated carrots can be thawed and made into carrot fritters, rice pilaf, or added to veggie ragu, or veggie lasagna. They can also be used in baking, such as carrot cake or carrot muffins.

CANNING YOUR CARROTS

You can preserve carrots through **pressure canning** for use in soups, stews, favourite carrot recipes, or as a side. Peel first, then slice or dice. Pack raw or boiled (5 min). Pressure canning steps, pg 57
Processing time: 25 min (pints) 30 min (quarts)

DEHYDRATING YOUR CARROTS

Carrots take around 6-12 hours to dehydrate, depending on their thickness. Slice thinly, shred or small dice. Blanch first (if desired, pg 48) to extend shelf life. Dehydrating steps, pg 63

TO USE: Enjoy dehydrated carrots as a crunchy snack. Add them with nuts for a custom trail mix. They can also be rehydrated and added to soups, stews, or casseroles. Or mixed with rice, quinoa, or couscous for your favourite side dishes. Grind them into powder for natural orange food colouring.

FERMENTING YOUR CARROTS

Fermenting carrots creates a probiotic-rich, tangy condiment that can be used in salads, sandwiches, mixed into dips and sauces, or as a side dish. Shred, slice, or dice. Fermenting steps, pg 74

TO USE: Chopped or shredded fermented carrots can be added to salads, wraps, or sandwiches for a burst of flavour and probiotics. Blend them with other ingredients like (onions, mustard, and vinegar) to create a tasty carrot relish for hot dogs or sandwiches. Purée fermented carrots and mix them into sauces, salad dressings, hummus, or vinaigrettes for added depth, colour and nutrition. Or serve fermented carrots as a tangy side dish alongside roasted or grilled meats and vegetables.

PICKLING YOUR CARROTS

Carrots can be plain pickled or flavoured in any number of sweet or savoury pickle variations (such as honey + ginger pickled, curry pickled, dill pickled, spicy pickled) to enjoy throughout the year. Pickling steps, pg 80 or 81
Processing time (water bath canning):15 min

TO USE: Pickled carrots are a delicious pantry treat enjoyed straight from the jar, served alongside charcuterie or cheese boards, on burgers, sandwiches, or hot dogs, or for adding delicious zing in salads.

CELERIAC

Bulbous winter root vegetable with subtle celery flavour.

 Leaves are edible with a parsley-like flavour but tend to be coarse and are typically discarded. The pale, younger leaves will have a more delicate texture. You can use them chopped up as fresh seasoning in salads, pesto (pg 39), or cooked into soups and stews.

 Celery-like stalks are edible, though are more fibrous and woody than regular celery. Choose the more tender, young stalks to enjoy, or simply discard them.

 Root is wonderful chopped, grated, mashed, sautéed, and cooked into those fall soups, stews, or roasts. First peel away the brown outer skin with a vegetable peeler to reveal the white edible center.

FRESH STORAGE Remove leafy stems from the root (they draw moisture away from it). Store stalks and roots separately in sealed bags or containers in refrigerator. Stalks and leaves last 1-2 weeks, roots last up to 6 months.

QUIRKS Browning of the flesh occurs once peeled or cut and comes in contact with air (oxidation). To minimize browning, use promptly after cutting or peeling, or submerge in water until ready to use. Store cut celeriac in a container of water in the refrigerator and ensure it is completely submerged. Change the water if it becomes cloudy.

PRESERVATION Freeze, dehydrate or pickle.
Be sure to blanch first as celeriac rapidly browns (pg 48).
(See next page for more)

Celeriac leaves can also be preserved through dehydrating and turning into powder for added nutrition in recipes, or made into pesto and frozen (pg 39).

FREEZING YOUR CELERIAC

Celeriac is best frozen blanched or cooked (pg 48).
Freezing it raw will significantly diminish the texture and flavour. Cube, slice, or grate it, then blanch it (pg 48). Alternatively, you can steam, boil, roast, or sauté it until it reaches your desired level of cooking. Allow to cool, then portion and package.

TO USE: Can cook directly from frozen or thaw it in the refrigerator before incorporating into your recipes. Cubes of celeriac can be roasted straight from the freezer; simply toss with olive oil and a sprinkle of salt. Frozen cooked celeriac can be used in a wide variety of dishes, including soups, mashes, casseroles, fritters, and gratins.

CANNING It is not recommended to pressure can celeriac.

DEHYDRATING YOUR CELERIAC

Celeriac takes around 4-12 hours to dehydrate, depending on thickness. Peel. Slice thinly, shred, or small dice. Soak 5 minutes in lemon water (optional) to prevent browning (1 tsp lemon juice per 1 cup water). Dehydrating steps, pg 63

TO USE: Enjoy dehydrated celeriac chips as a crunchy snack, or you can grind them into a powder as a flavour addition for recipes. Dehydrated celeriac can also be rehydrated and added to soups, stew, casseroles, or risottos.

PICKLING YOUR CELERIAC

Celeriac can be pickled for long-term storage. Peel first, then slice or cube. Pickling steps, pg 80 or 81 **Processing time (water bath canning): 15 min**

TO USE: Use pickled celeriac as a topping on sandwiches, salads, tacos, grain bowls, sushi rolls or cold noodle dishes.

PARSNIP

—

Long, tapered root vegetable with sweet, nutty flavour.

 Leaves and stalks contain a **toxic** sap. They can cause irritation, rash and blistering of the skin, as well as abdominal symptoms and kidney issues if ingested. When handling tops, be sure to wear gloves. Discard them.

 Root is delicious raw or cooked. It is sweetest roasted but can also be boiled, fried, steamed, puréed, or added to cozy fall soups and stews. It is best peeled and the stem trimmed before use. Mature parsnips will also have a woody core—remove this by slicing the vegetable into quarters lengthwise and cutting out the dark, distinguishable core.

FRESH STORAGE	Remove leafy stems and discard them (wear gloves when handling parsnip tops). Store in sealed bags or containers in refrigerator. They will last a couple of weeks.
QUIRKS	Browning of the flesh occurs once peeled or cut and comes in contact with air (oxidation). To minimize this, use promptly after cutting or peeling, or submerge in water until ready to use to limit their exposure to air. Store cut parsnips in a container of water in the refrigerator and ensure they are completely submerged. Change the water if it becomes cloudy.
PRESERVATION	Freeze, pressure can, dehydrate, ferment, or pickle. (See next page for more)

FREEZING YOUR PARSNIPS

You can freeze your parsnips raw, blanched, or cooked (pg 48).
Freeze them chopped, grated, or puréed, depending on your purpose. **Freeze purée in pre-portioned amounts** (such as 1 cup or 2 cups) based on what you plan to use it for.

TO USE: Can cook directly from frozen.
Roast them or add them directly to cooking such as soups, stews, casseroles, pot pies or gratins. Grated or puréed parsnips can be thawed and used in baking such as cakes or muffins.

CANNING YOUR PARSNIPS

You can preserve parsnips through **pressure canning** for use in recipes. Peel first, then dice or slice into uniform pieces. Boil for 3 minutes before packing into jars. Pressure canning steps, pg 57   **Processing time: 30 min (pints) 35 min (quarts)**

DEHYDRATING YOUR PARSNIPS

Parsnips take around 4-12 hours to dehydrate, depending on their thickness. Slice thinly, shred or small dice. Soak 5 minutes in lemon water (optional) to prevent browning (1 tsp lemon juice per 1 cup water). Dehydrating steps, pg 63

TO USE: Enjoy dehydrated parsnips as a crunchy snack. They can also be rehydrated and added to soups, stews, casseroles, mashes, pot pies, or risottos.

FERMENTING YOUR PARSNIPS

Fermented parsnips develop a unique tangy flavour and are a great, probiotic-rich addition to your homemade dishes. Shred, slice, or dice. Fermenting steps, pg 74

TO USE: Fermented parsnips can be enjoyed as a tangy side dish, a snack, or as an ingredient in various recipes. They pair well with salads, sandwiches, wraps, in grain bowls, or alongside charcuterie boards. They can also be used as a topper on burgers or hot dogs or alongside meat dishes (such as roast chicken or pork) to add a tangy contrast.

PICKLING YOUR PARSNIPS

Parsnips can be plain pickled or flavoured in any number of sweet or savoury pickle variations (such as honey + ginger pickled, curry pickled, dill pickled, spicy pickled) to enjoy throughout the year. Pickling steps, pg 80 or 81 **Processing time (water bath canning):15 min**

TO USE: Pickled parsnips have a unique and tangy flavour. They are a delicious pantry treat enjoyed straight from the jar, served alongside charcuterie or cheese boards, as part of hors d'oeuvres, on pulled pork or barbecue sandwiches, tacos, or grilled fish.

POTATO

Starchy, edible tuber with quiet, earthy flavour.

 Potatoes are eaten cooked. The entire potato, skin and flesh, is edible. The skin has more nutrients than the potato interior, so potatoes are best for you with the skin left on. When peeling your potatoes, the peels can be made into potato peel chips. Enjoy your potatoes baked, roasted, mashed, parboiled, fried, or added to soups, stews, or potato salad.

FRESH STORAGE — Store unwashed (if washed, allow to fully dry first) in a cool, dry, dark place such as a pantry, back of a cupboard, or garage. Do not store in plastic, rather keep them in a basket, burlap sack, or crate so the air can circulate around them. Cover with a towel to protect them from light, and store them away from apples, bananas, and onions (these ethylene-producing items will accelerate rotting). If any spuds become soft, shrivelled, or musty smelling, toss them. Lasts 2-3 months.

QUIRKS — Browning of the flesh occurs rapidly once the potato has been peeled or cut and comes in contact with air (oxidation). To minimize browning, use potatoes promptly after cutting or peeling, or submerge them in water until ready to use to limit their exposure to air. Store cut potatoes in a container of water in the refrigerator and ensure they are completely submerged. Change the water if it becomes cloudy.

PRESERVATION — Freeze, pressure can, or dehydrate.
(See next page for more)

Types of Potatoes

There are many varieties of potatoes, each with their own unique qualities.
When cooking, your choice of potato will significantly impact the taste, texture, and overall success of your dish, so it's important to choose the right type. Here are the main types of potatoes and their traits:

Waxy	Firm and smooth texture with higher moisture content and lower starch content. **Best for salads, soups, and dishes where you want the potato to hold its shape.** (E.g. New potatoes, Fingerling, and Yukon Gold)
Starchy	Dry, mealy texture and a high starch content, tend to break down more easily when cooked. **Best for baking, mashing, and frying due to their fluffy texture when cooked.** (E.g. Russet, Idaho, King Edward, and Maris Piper)
Creamy	Known for their smooth and buttery texture, making them **ideal for mashed potatoes**. (E.g. Yukon Gold, Yellow Finn, and Red Gold)
All-purpose	Falling between waxy and starchy varieties, these potatoes are a go-to choice for recipes as they are versatile and **work well for most cooking methods.** (E.g. Yukon Gold, Kennebec, and Purple Majesty)
Fingerling	Small, slender, and elongated with a waxy texture, coming in various colours, they are prized for their unique appearance and flavour and **most commonly roasted.** (E.g. Russian Banana, French Fingerling, and Purple Peruvian)
Specialty	Varieties with unique colours, flavours, or textures like having blue, red, streaked, or purple flesh. Prepared in various ways, these are typically **used to elevate the visual and gustatory appeal of dishes**. (E.g. Purple Majesty, All Blue, and Adirondack Blue)

A note about NEW POTATOES

New potatoes are a tender, delicate, early summer treat, not to be confused with small or baby potatoes. They are "new" because they have not yet developed a skin. They are only around for the first few weeks of summer and are much sweeter because they have not matured enough yet for their sugar to develop into starch.

Handle them gently, and keep them in the refrigerator crisper as they spoil easily.

FREEZING YOUR POTATOES

You can freeze your potatoes blanched or cooked. It is **not** recommended to freeze them raw. Freeze them whole, sliced, diced, or even mashed (peeled or unpeeled), depending on your purpose. Blanching times depend on how large your potato pieces are (3 minutes for hash browns, 5 minutes for chopped, 10 minutes for whole; see pg 48)

NOTE: Certain potato varieties will freeze better than others. The best potatoes for freezing are those with lower moisture content (such as Russet, Yukon Gold, Katahdin, and Kennebec), as the water freezes, and when thawed, certain varieties will become mushy and grainy.

TO USE: Can cook directly from frozen.
Frozen potatoes can be a convenient way to have ingredients on hand for various dishes, such as soups, stews, or casseroles. You can also **pre-make your own french fries, potato wedges, or hash browns** and have them ready to go from frozen.

CANNING YOUR POTATOES

You can preserve potatoes through pressure canning. Peel first, then chop, slice, or leave whole. Boil for 2 min (for 1/2" dice), 5 minutes (for chunks), and 10 minutes (for whole potatoes) before packing into jars and covering with fresh boiling water. (Do not use the water you boiled the potatoes with; it contains too much starch. Do not can mashed potatoes; they are too thick, and it becomes hazardous.) Pressure canning steps, pg 57
Processing time: 35 min (pints) 40 min (quarts)

DEHYDRATING YOUR POTATOES

Potatoes take around 6-12 hours to dehydrate, depending on their thickness and moisture content. Slice thinly or small dice. Blanch 5 minutes first. Dehydrating steps, pg 63

TO USE: Rehydrate potatoes by soaking them in warm water for about 15-30 minutes or by adding them directly to soups, stews, or casseroles during cooking. You can also use rehydrated potatoes to make mashed potatoes, scalloped potatoes, hash browns, potato pancakes, gnocchi, and curries, or add them to frittata.

RADISHES
—

Crunchy, fast-growing root vegetable with peppery flavour.

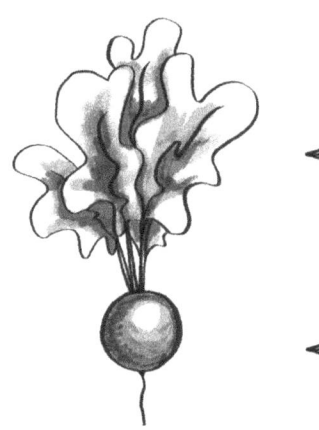

Tops are edible and delicious. They do have a fuzzy, unpleasant texture, but this goes away when cooked. Try them sautéed with a bit of oil and garlic and a squeeze of lemon, substitute them for spinach or greens in cooking recipes, add them to smoothies, or make radish top pesto (pg 39).

Root is most often eaten raw. Slice thinly and add on sandwiches, tacos, or salads, or serve halved with a smear of butter and a sprinkle of salt. They are also delicious pickled or roasted. Once cooked, they soften and develop a more mellow flavour.

FRESH STORAGE	Remove leafy stems from radishes (they draw moisture away from the root), leaving a small portion of stems attached. Store leaves and roots separately in sealed bags or containers in refrigerator. Wash leaves when ready to use. Leaves last up to 1 week, roots last for weeks.
QUICK TIP	Radishes pair well with ingredients like butter, cheese, yogurt, dill, mint, citrus, and other fresh herbs. Experiment with flavours, as well as different radish varieties, to find your favourite combo.
PRESERVATION	Freeze, dehydrate, ferment, or pickle. (See next page for more) Radish tops can also be preserved through freezing, dehydrating, turning into powder for added nutrition in recipes, or made into pesto and frozen (pg 39). Follow methods for spinach (pg 204).

FREEZING YOUR RADISHES

You can freeze your radishes blanched or cooked, but be prepared for a softer texture once thawed. Freeze them whole, halved, quartered, or already roasted, depending on your purpose. (Blanching instructions, pg 48)
It is **not recommended** to freeze them raw as they will turn to mush when thawed.

TO USE: Use in roasted or baked dishes.

CANNING It is not recommended to pressure can radishes.

DEHYDRATING YOUR RADISHES

Radishes take around 3-12 hours to dehydrate, depending on their thickness. No blanching is needed. Dehydrating steps, pg 63

TO USE: Enjoy dehydrated radishes as a crunchy snack, as a topping for salads and soups, or as a flavorful addition to dishes like stir-fries or casseroles. They retain a concentrated radish flavour and are a convenient way to add a burst of taste and texture to your recipes.

FERMENTING YOUR RADISHES

Fermenting radishes produces delicious and tangy results. It enhances their flavour and introduces probiotics, which benefit gut health. Fermenting steps, pg 74

TO USE: Fermented radishes are often used in salads, tacos, sandwiches, in rice bowls, alongside grilled meats (such as chicken, pork, or beef), or served with cheese and crackers for a tangy, savoury appetizer.

PICKLING YOUR RADISHES

Pickled radishes add a bright burst of colour and flavour to dishes! They can be plain pickled or made in any number of sweet or savoury variations (such as sweet pickled, dill pickled, spicy pickled). Pickling steps, pg 80 or 81
Processing time (water bath canning):10 min

TO USE: Pickled radishes are a delicious condiment on burgers, sandwiches, tacos, or hot dogs. They also add a brilliant zing to salads, grain or rice bowls, in sushi rolls, alongside barbecue dishes or grilled meats, with seafood, or as a bright and tangy contrast with roasted vegetables.

RUTABAGA
—

Firm, dense root vegetable with mild, lightly sweet flavour.

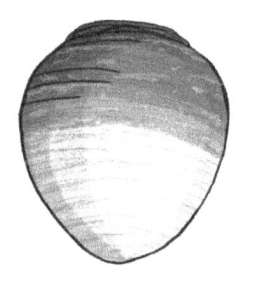

Typically trimmed of leaves and stems before you receive them. Leaves are edible, though are coarse raw. Having a hearty texture, they are best cooked. Use them similar to how you would collard greens (pg 180). Remove woody stems and discard.

Root can be eaten raw (added to salads) but is typically cooked. Skin is best peeled. Creamy yellow flesh can be enjoyed mashed with potatoes or other root vegetables, cubed and added to soups, stews, casseroles, gratins, or breakfast hash. It is delicious roasted, which enhances its natural sweetness and gives it a delightful caramelized flavor. Pair with other autumn root vegetables for a delicious fall bake.

FRESH STORAGE	Remove leafy stems and taproot if not already removed. Store in a sealed plastic bag in the refrigerator. Lasts for months.
QUICK TIP	Rutabaga pairs best with other root vegetables (such as carrots, parsnip, potatoes, celeriac, and turnip) and ingredients like rosemary, thyme, butter, onions, leeks, celery, and nutmeg.
PRESERVATION	Freeze, dehydrate, ferment, or pickle. (See next page for more) Rutabaga tops can be preserved using the same methods as for collard greens (pg 182).

FREEZING YOUR RUTABAGA

You can freeze your rutabaga raw, blanched, or cooked (pg 48).
Freeze it chopped, grated, mashed, puréed, or sliced, depending on your purpose. I recommend peeling it first to improve texture and flavour.

TO USE: Can cook directly from frozen.
Frozen rutabaga can be used in various dishes such as soups, stews, casseroles, mashes, shepherd's pie, grain bowls, or roasted as a side.

CANNING It is not recommended to pressure can rutabaga.

DEHYDRATING YOUR RUTABAGA

Rutabaga takes around 6-12 hours to dehydrate, depending on thickness. Peel and slice thinly. Dehydrating steps, pg 63

TO USE: Dehydrated rutabaga chips can be used as a crunchy snack or added to soups, stews, gratins, and casseroles. Rehydrate rutabaga pieces by soaking them in warm water.

FERMENTING YOUR RUTABAGA

Rutabaga can be fermented into a probiotic-rich, tangy side (much like sauerkraut or kimchi) that can be used in salads, sandwiches, or on its own. Peel first, then grate or slice, mixing with additional vegetables, spices or herbs if desired. Fermenting steps, pg 74

TO USE: Add fermented rutabaga to salads, wraps, sandwiches, or grain bowls for a burst of flavour and probiotics. Serve alongside cheese and crackers for a flavorful appetizer or snack (its tangy taste complements the creamy richness of cheese and the crunch of crackers). Use as a garnish for soups or stews, or add to tacos for a nutritious filling.

PICKLING YOUR RUTABAGA

Rutabaga can be plain pickled or flavoured in any number of variations (such as spicy pickled, ginger pickled, apple + mustard seed pickled) to enjoy throughout the year. Peel first, cut into sticks or slice into rounds. Pickling steps, pg 80 or 81
Processing time (water bath canning):10 min

TO USE: Pickled rutabaga is a tangy, crunchy condiment you can use in sandwiches, wraps, hot dogs, or tacos. Serve alongside barbecue and grilled meats. They also add a brilliant zing to salads, grain bowls, or alongside charcuterie or cheese boards.

SWEET POTATO
—

Large edible root with sweet, caramel-like flavour.

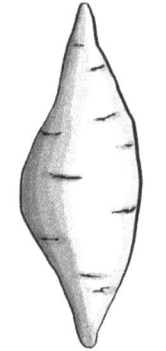

Sweet potatoes are eaten cooked. Entire potato is edible, skin and flesh. The skin has more nutrients than the potato interior, so sweet potatoes are best for you with skin left on, however they are often peeled for recipes. Enjoy your sweet potatoes baked, roasted, mashed, fried, or added to soups, stews, or hashes.

FRESH STORAGE — Store unwashed in a cool, dry, dark place such as a pantry, back of a cupboard, or garage. Do not store in plastic, instead keep them in a basket, burlap sack, or crate so the air can circulate around them. Cover with a towel to protect them from light, and store them away from apples, bananas, and onions (these ethylene producing items will accelerate rotting). If any become soft, shrivelled, or musty smelling, toss them. Lasts 2-3 months.

QUIRKS — Browning of the flesh occurs once the sweet potato has been peeled or cut and comes in contact with air (oxidation). To minimize browning, use it promptly after cutting or peeling, or submerge it in water until ready to use to limit the exposure to air. Store cut sweet potatoes in a container of water in the refrigerator and ensure they are completely submerged. Change the water if it becomes cloudy.

PRESERVATION — Freeze, pressure can, dehydrate.
(See next page for more)

A note about SWEET POTATO vs YAM

Often mislabelled, yams and sweet potatoes are not the same thing. That orange candied yam bake you love to eat at Thanksgiving is not yam at all- it is sweet potato. Grocery stores and packaging commonly mislabel this item, and those beloved recipes passed down often mention the wrong ingredient.

Yams are white inside, so the orange flesh alone tells you it is a sweet potato you are working with (sweet potatoes also come in purple and white). Other differences include the taste (sweet potatoes have a much sweeter flavour, whereas yams are more neutral tasting), the skin (sweet potatoes have smooth orange or reddish skin with eyes like potatoes, whereas yams have a rough brown skin like tree bark with fine root hairs), and the size (yams can grow much larger than sweet potatoes, up to 5 ft long). Yams aren't available in most North American grocery stores, so most of us have never seen one.

FREEZING YOUR SWEET POTATOES

You can freeze your sweet potatoes blanched or cooked (pg 48).
It is **not** recommended to freeze them raw. Freeze them whole, sliced, diced, or even mashed (peeled or unpeeled), depending on your purpose.

TO USE: Can cook directly from frozen.
Frozen potatoes can be a convenient ingredient to have on hand for a variety of dishes, such as soups, stews, casseroles, curries, enchiladas, or grain bowls. You can also **pre-make your own sweet potato fries, wedges, or cubes** and cook them right from frozen.

CANNING YOUR SWEET POTATOES

You can preserve sweet potatoes through **pressure canning**, but note that preserving them will make them soft (plan to use them mashed or puréed afterward). Peel and cut into uniform chunks. Boil for 3 minutes before packing into jars. You can choose to cover them in hot water or hot syrup. Hot water is the simpler option, but hot syrup (made with water and sugar) enhances their flavor. Pressure canning steps, pg 57
Processing time: 65 min (pints) 90 min (quarts)

DEHYDRATING YOUR SWEET POTATOES

Sweet potatoes take around 6-12 hours to dehydrate, depending on their thickness. Slice thinly, shred or small dice. Pre-treat by baking for 10 minutes at 350° before transferring to trays for dehydration. Dehydrating steps, pg 63

TO USE: Dehydrated sweet potatoes make a delicious nutritious snack! Season them with cinnamon, salt, or other spices before dehydrating. Combine dehydrated sweet potatoes with nuts, seeds, and dried fruits to create a flavorful trail mix. Rehydrate sweet potatoes by soaking them in warm water for about 15-30 minutes or by adding them directly to soups, stews, curries, or casseroles during cooking. You can also use rehydrated pieces as an oatmeal topping, added to your grain bowls, or as a delicious side.

TURNIPS

Firm, crunchy root vegetable with peppery notes.

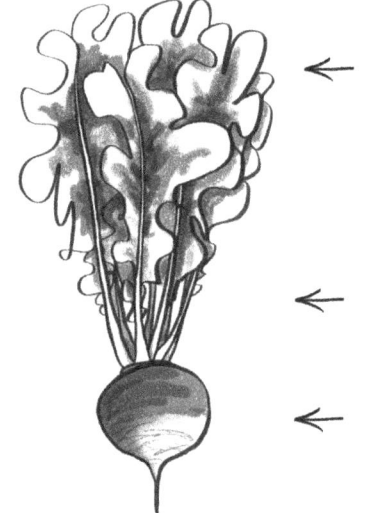

← Leaves are edible and delicious, especially earlier in the season. They are also highly nutritious. They can be substituted for spinach or swiss chard in recipes, are wonderful braised, sautéed, added to eggs or omelets, in smoothies, pestos (pg 39), or in sandwiches. Later in season, they do take on a stronger, more peppery, bitter flavour.

← Stems should be discarded, as they are fibrous and unpleasant.

← Root is delicious raw (when young and sweet) or cooked. Later season turnips become stronger flavoured. Turnips are an ideal potato replacement as they have a similar texture while being more nutrient rich, and can be substituted in dishes such as gratins, mashes, or even french fries. Roasting will enhance their natural sweetness and gives them a delightful caramelized flavour. Larger turnips are best peeled.

FRESH STORAGE — Remove leafy stems from turnip (they draw moisture away from the root) leaving a small portion of stems attached. Discard stems, store leaves and roots separately in sealed bags or containers in refrigerator. Wash leaves when ready to use. Leaves last a week, roots last for weeks.

PRESERVATION — Freeze, pressure can, dehydrate, ferment, or pickle.
(See next page for more)

Turnip tops can also be preserved through freezing, dehydrating, turning into powder for added nutrition in recipes, or made into pesto (pg 39) and frozen. Follow methods for spinach (pg 204).

FREEZING YOUR TURNIPS

You can freeze your turnips raw, blanched, or cooked (pg 48).
Freeze them chopped, grated, puréed, or sliced, depending on your purpose.
Sweet summer turnips don't need any peeling first, but winter turnips (larger ones) should be peeled first to improve their texture and flavour.

TO USE: Can cook directly from frozen.
Frozen turnips can be a convenient ingredient to have on hand for various dishes such as soups, stews, casseroles, mashes, shepherd's pie, grain bowls, or roasted right from frozen.

CANNING YOUR TURNIPS

You can preserve turnips through **pressure canning** for use in soups, stews, casseroles, or roasts. Peel first. Pack raw or boiled (3 min). Pressure canning steps, pg 57
Processing time: 30 min (pints) 35 min (quarts)

DEHYDRATING YOUR TURNIPS

Turnips take around 6-12 hours to dehydrate, depending on their thickness. Peel and slice thinly. Blanch for 3 minutes. Dehydrating steps, pg 63

TO USE: Dehydrated turnips can be used as a crunchy snack, or used in soups, stews, gratins, casseroles. Rehydrate turnips by soaking them in warm water, and use them in pasta or rice dishes, or cassoulet.

FERMENTING YOUR TURNIPS

Fermenting turnips creates a probiotic-rich, tangy condiment that can be used in salads, sandwiches, or as a side. Peel first, then grate or slice. Fermenting steps, pg 74

TO USE: Add fermented turnips to salads, wraps, tacos, or sandwiches for a burst of flavour and probiotics. Use in rice or grain bowls, in sushi, or alongside Middle Eastern dishes (such as falafel, hummus, or kebabs).

PICKLING YOUR TURNIPS

Pickled turnips are known for their tangy flavour and crisp texture. Turnips can be plain pickled or flavoured in any number of sweet or savoury variations (such as ginger + turmeric pickled, honey mustard pickled, cumin + coriander pickled) to enjoy throughout the year. Peel first. Pickling steps, pg 80 or 81
Processing time (water bath canning):10 min

TO USE: Pickled turnips are a delicious condiment on sandwiches, wraps, or tacos. They also add a brilliant zing to salads, grain or rice bowls, in sushi rolls, or on a mezze or charcuterie platter. They pair well with Middle Eastern or Mediterranean dishes (falafel, shawarma, or kebabs), or alongside grilled meats.

STEMS

Vegetables // grown for their stem

ASPARAGUS
—

Long, pointy spears with leafy flavour.

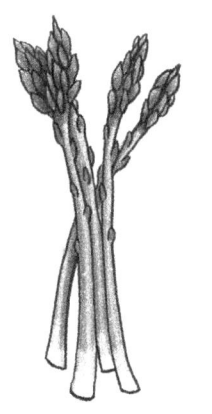

 Tender tips and fleshy stems are edible. They can be eaten raw in salads or steamed, sautéed, roasted, or grilled. Add to stir fries, risottos, frittata or quiche, blanched and added to wraps, or pickled. They are a quick cooking vegetable.

 Woody stem at the bottom is tough to eat and typically removed. Snap or cut bottom portion (1-2") off and discard.

FRESH STORAGE	Store asparagus as you would fresh-cut flowers. Trim bottoms and stand up in a glass jar with an inch of water to hydrate and keep stalks crisp. Cover with a plastic bag and refrigerate. Lasts a week.
QUICK TIP	Asparagus is a quick-cooking vegetable, taking only a few minutes until done. Overcooked asparagus becomes bland and mushy. You want it to be tender crisp. Pan fry it in oil for 3-4 minutes, blanch in boiling water for 1-3 minutes, or roast it (drizzled in olive oil) for 10-12 minutes for a perfect side. Sprinkle with salt and pepper or toss with freshly grated parmesan, olive oil, and lemon zest.
PRESERVATION	Freeze, pressure can, dehydrate, ferment, or pickle. (See next page for more)

FREEZING YOUR ASPARAGUS

You can freeze your asparagus blanched or cooked (pg 48).
Trim the ends and freeze them whole or chopped, depending on your purpose.
It is **not recommended** to freeze them raw as they will turn mealy and mushy when thawed.

TO USE: Can cook directly from frozen.
You can add frozen asparagus directly too soups, stews and casseroles. Throw in stir fries, quiches, frittatas, pasta dishes, or risottos. You can also grill or roast frozen asparagus for a delicious side.

CANNING YOUR ASPARAGUS

You can preserve asparagus through **pressure canning**. Pack raw into jars (leaving 1" headspace). Pressure canning steps, pg 57
Processing time: 30 min (pints) 40 min (quarts)

DEHYDRATING YOUR ASPARAGUS

Asparagus takes around 4-12 hours to dehydrate, depending on its thickness and moisture content. Cut asparagus into 3-4 inch pieces. Blanch for 4 minutes. Dehydrating steps, pg 63

TO USE: Dehydrated asparagus can be rehydrated by soaking it in warm water for 15 minutes before use or added directly to soups and stews during cooking. Use in casseroles, pasta dishes, egg dishes, risotto, vegetable medleys, and grain bowls.

FERMENTING YOUR ASPARAGUS

Fermenting asparagus imparts a unique tangy flavour and can result in a crunchy and lightly sour probiotic vegetable. Trim ends, chop or leave whole. Fermenting steps, pg 74

TO USE: Fermented asparagus can be used in salads, wraps, in omelets or frittatas, pasta dishes, rice bowls, dips or spreads, in sushi rolls, or as a cocktail garnish.

PICKLING YOUR ASPARAGUS

Asparagus can be plain pickled or flavoured in any number of savoury pickle variations (such as mustard seed pickled, smoky pickled, spicy pickled) to enjoy throughout the year. Trim ends, chop or leave whole. Pickling steps, pg 80 or 81
Processing time (water bath canning):10 min

TO USE: Pickled asparagus is a delicious pantry treat enjoyed straight from the jar, served on antipasto platters, charcuterie boards, or as a Bloody Mary garnish. Mix in pasta salads, egg dishes, sushi rolls, dips and spreads, in quiches or savoury tarts, or on grilled cheese sandwiches.

BOK CHOY

Thick, clustered stalks and leaves with tender, juicy flavour.

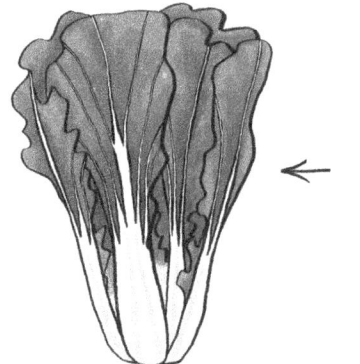

This entire plant is edible with thick, clustered stalks that are crunchy yet juicy, and lush green leaves having a mild, spinach-like flavour. All parts quick cook to be beautifully tender. Commonly used in Asian cooking, the favourite ways to eat this vegetable are: braised, steamed, roasted, stir-fried, added to ramen, or served with rice or fish.

FRESH STORAGE Store whole in a sealed bag or container in refrigerator. Lasts up to 2 weeks.

QUIRKS All parts cook quickly, requiring only a few minutes until done. Overcooked bok choy becomes soggy and mushy. You want it tender crisp. Pan fry it in oil for 2 minutes, steam it for 2-3 minutes, roast (halved or quartered) for 10 minutes. Add at the end of cooking to soups, stir fries and other recipes.

PRESERVATION Freeze, dehydrate, ferment, or pickle.
(See next page for more)

FREEZING YOUR BOK CHOY

You can freeze your bok choy raw (pg 48).
Raw freezing gives best results, blanching or cooking creates a mushy product once thawed. Freeze them chopped up, ready for use. Note that it will have a softer texture after freezing that is best used in cooked dishes.

TO USE: Can cook directly from frozen.
Frozen bok choy can be used in stir fries, soups, stews, curries, fried rice, or various Asian-inspired dishes.

CANNING It is not recommended to pressure can bok choy.

DEHYDRATING YOUR BOK CHOY

Bok choy takes around 4-10 hours to dehydrate, depending on thickness. Separate leaves from stems. Leaves can be dehydrated whole (they break apart on their own), stems should be sliced thinly. Dehydrating steps, pg 63

TO USE: Dehydrated bok choy can be rehydrated by soaking it in warm water for 15 minutes before use or added directly to soups and stews during cooking. Enjoy in noodle bowls, quiches, frittatas, or stir fries.

FERMENTING YOUR BOK CHOY

You can ferment your bok choy to use in salads, wraps, or grain bowls. Another popular way is to make kimchi, a traditional Korean fermented vegetable dish. Kimchi often includes napa cabbage, but you can use bok choy as a substitute or in combination with other vegetables. Fermenting steps, pg 74

TO USE: Make kimchi fried rice, kimchi pancakes, kimchi ramen or noodle soup, kimchi quesadillas or grilled cheese, or kimchi stir fry.

PICKLING YOUR BOK CHOY

Bok choy can be plain pickled or flavoured in any number of sweet or savoury pickle variations (such as sesame ginger pickled, mustard seed pickled, sweet and sour pickled) to enjoy during the year. Pickling steps, pg 80 or 81
Processing time (water bath canning):10 min

TO USE: Pickled bok choy can add a burst of tangy and crunchy flavour to a variety of dishes. Layer in sandwiches or wraps, as a burger topper, or chop it up and toss it in salads. Add pickled bok choy to rice bowls. noodle dishes, poke bowls, stir fries, or mix it into a dip for dumplings or spring rolls.

CELERY
—

Marshland plant with bright green, crunchy stalks.

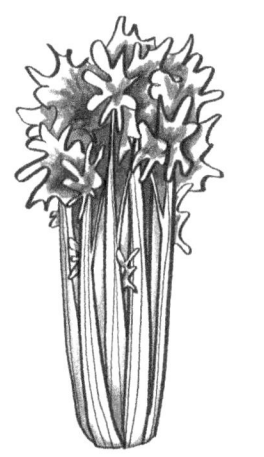

 Leaves are edible with a parsley-like flavour, though they tend to be coarse. The pale, younger leaves will have a more delicate texture. You can use them chopped up as fresh seasoning in salads, made into celery powder, celery oil, pestos, or cooked into soups, stews and stuffings.

 Stalks are delicious, they can be eaten raw or cooked. Great for snacking, celery adds crunch and a pleasing mild flavour to salads, soups, stuffings, and stews.

FRESH STORAGE — If possible, keep celery heads whole until use, as they will retain their water better. Store in a sealed bag or container in the refrigerator. Lasts up to four weeks.

QUIRKS — Celery was originally discovered growing in marshes. This vegetable has high water content and likes to be kept hydrated. If your head is drying out or going limp, it can be reinvigorated by trimming 1/2" off the bottom and placed in a jar or vase of cold water for a few hours to overnight in the refrigerator. Once it is good as new, return to sealed bag or container. (Celery that has been cut into sticks can be immersed in a tray of cold water to rehydrate.)

PRESERVATION — Freeze, dehydrate, ferment, or pickle.
(See next page for more)

Celery leaves can also be preserved through freezing or dehydrating and ground into powder (pg 63) for added flavour and nutrition in recipes.

FREEZING YOUR CELERY

You can freeze your celery raw, blanched, or cooked (pg 48).
Blanching will extend its freezer life. Freeze it chopped, ready for use. Freezing **will cause celery to become limp** when thawed, suitable only for cooked dishes like soups, stews, stuffings, and casseroles.

TO USE: Cook directly from frozen.
Use in soups, stews, chili, stuffings, casseroles, sauces or gravies, or in rice dishes. Keep in mind that the texture will be softened compared to fresh cooked celery.

CANNING It is not recommended to pressure can celery.

DEHYDRATING YOUR CELERY

Celery takes around 4-12 hours to dehydrate, depending on thickness and moisture content. Slice thinly. Blanch 1 minute first. Dehydrating steps, pg 63

TO USE: Dehydrated celery can be rehydrated by soaking it in warm water for 15 minutes before use or added directly to soups and stews during cooking. It's a great way to have celery on hand for dishes when fresh celery isn't readily available. Use in casseroles or rice pilafs. Dehydrated celery can also be ground into powder and used in homemade seasoning blends (pg 67), meat rubs and marinades, or salad dressings.

FERMENTING YOUR CELERY

Fermented celery can be a tasty and probiotic-rich addition to your diet. Chop or cut into sticks. Fermenting steps, pg 74

TO USE: Fermented celery can be used in salads and sandwiches, or eaten as a side dish. Use in sushi rolls, stir fries, as a garnish for soups and stews, or in rice bowls.

PICKLING YOUR CELERY

Celery can be plain pickled or flavoured in any number of sweet or savoury pickle variations (such as italian herb pickled, dill pickled, spicy pickled) to enjoy throughout the year. Chop or cut into sticks. Pickling steps, pg 80 or 81
Processing time (water bath canning):10 min

TO USE: Pickled celery can be used in salads, sandwiches, tacos, or enjoyed as a crunchy and zesty snack. You can also mix it in your egg salad or chicken salad, chopped up and mixed into dips and spreads, or incorporated into rice or grain bowls.

FENNEL
—

Firm, crunchy bulb with perfumy, licorice flavour.

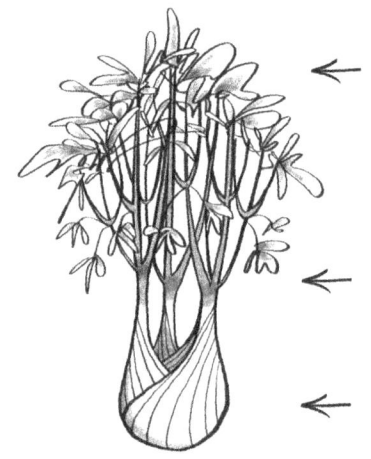

← Feathery green fronds melt in your mouth with a delightfully delicate flavour. Think of them as light herbs that are best used fresh. Strip fronds from stalks and toss them in salads, on sandwiches, or sprinkle over roasted vegetables or fish.

← Stalks are fibrous and inedible, though they do add delicious flavour to soups, broths, or sauces before tossing.

← Bulb is delicious raw or cooked. It adds bright, fresh flavour to salads or slaws. It is often shaved or sliced thinly, sauteed, roasted, or pickled. It is also delicious chopped, then caramelized, grilled, or braised until tender.

FRESH STORAGE — Remove stalks from the bulb (they draw moisture away from it). Store fronds and bulb separately in sealed bags or containers in refrigerator. Fronds will last a week, bulb lasts for many weeks.

QUICK TIP — Fennel pairs well with pork, chicken or fish, as well as ingredients like citrus, apples, fruits, seafood, herbs, and cheese.

PRESERVATION — Freeze, dehydrate, ferment, or pickle.
(See next page for more)

Fronds can also be frozen or air dried (hung upside down in bouquets; pg 63), then stored or turned into powder for added nutrition and seasoning in recipes.

FREEZING YOUR FENNEL

You can freeze your fennel raw, blanched, or cooked (pg 48).
Freeze them diced, shaved, or cut into wedges, depending on your purpose. Note that freezing causes a somewhat softer texture once thawed, so they are best used in cooked dishes. **You can raw freeze the stalks and fronds as well** for delicious use in soup broth.

TO USE: Can cook directly from frozen.
Frozen fennel can be roasted or sautéed as a side, added to risotto, frittata or quiche, served alongside fish, or in a vegetable medley. Add it to soups, stews, casseroles, sauces, stir fries, or rice dishes.

CANNING It is not recommended to pressure can fennel.

DEHYDRATING YOUR FENNEL

Fennel takes around 6-12 hours to dehydrate, depending on thickness and moisture content. Blanch the whole bulb for 90 seconds first. Pat dry, Slice thinly. Dehydrating steps, pg 63

TO USE: Dehydrated fennel can be ground into powder and used in homemade seasoning blends, meat rubs, or salad dressings. Combine dehydrated fennel with other herbs to create a fragrant herbal tea blend, or add to bread dough or savoury muffin or scone recipes for a boost of flavour. Dehydrated fennel can be rehydrated by soaking it in warm water for 15 minutes before use or added directly to soups and stews during cooking. It can be a versatile ingredient, adding a concentrated burst of flavour to various dishes.

FERMENTING YOUR FENNEL

Fermenting fennel is a wonderful way to enhance its flavour while also providing probiotic health benefits. Dice, shave, or slice into wedges. Fermenting steps, pg 74

TO USE: Fermented fennel can be used in salads, sandwiches, burgers or on charcuterie boards. Use in grain bowls, dips, alongside fish or meat, or as a garnish for soups.

PICKLING YOUR FENNEL

Fennel can be plain pickled or flavoured in any number of sweet or savoury pickle variations (such as minty pickled, citrus pickled, herb-infused pickled, spicy pickled) to enjoy throughout the year. Slice thinly. Pickling steps, pg 80 or 81
Processing time (water bath canning):10 min

TO USE: Pickled fennel is a delicious in green or grain salads, on burgers, sandwiches, tacos, or wraps. Served it on charcuterie or cheese boards, noodle bowls, or alongside fish, seafood dishes, or other meats. Chop it up and mix it into dips or spreads, add over egg dishes, or use as a cocktail garnish.

GARLIC SCAPES

Curly, flavourful, garlicky stalk from the garlic plant.

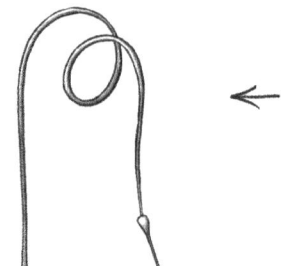

A vibrant seasonal delicacy (available only in early summer) with a delicious garlicky flavour. These beautiful, curly stalks are the flower bud of the garlic plant. Scapes are fantastic for grilling whole, sautéeing, roasting, pickling, or making into pesto. Chop them up and use them in recipes to add flavour to your cooking, similar to how you would use garlic.

FRESH STORAGE Store scapes in a sealed bag or container in refrigerator. Lasts up to 3 weeks.

PRESERVATION Freeze, dehydrate, ferment, or pickle.
(See next page for more)

You can also make and freeze garlic scape pesto (pg 39).

FREEZING YOUR GARLIC SCAPES

You can freeze your garlic scapes raw, blanched, or cooked (pg 48).
Freeze them whole, chopped or minced depending on your purpose. These freeze well. My favourite way is to chop them into small pieces and raw freeze for easy use.

TO USE: Can cook directly from frozen.
Use scapes to add garlicky flavour to your cooking, similar to how you would use garlic. You can also make and freeze batches of garlic scape pesto or garlic scape butter.

CANNING It is not recommended to pressure can garlic scapes.

DEHYDRATING YOUR GARLIC SCAPES

Garlic scapes take around 4-12 hours to dehydrate. Chop into small pieces. Dehydrating steps, pg 63

TO USE: Dehydrated garlic scapes can be ground into powder and used in homemade seasoning blends (pg 67), seasoning salt, meat rubs, or salad dressings. Or add them to soups, stews, bread dough or savoury muffin or scone recipes for a boost of flavour.

FERMENTING YOUR GARLIC SCAPES

Fermenting garlic scapes creates a probiotic-rich, tangy condiment. Pack in jar whole or chopped. Fermenting steps, pg 74

TO USE: Chop and add them to sauces, marinades, dips, and dressings. Use them as a condiment on burgers, as a pizza topping, or as a sandwich spread.

PICKLING YOUR GARLIC SCAPES

Garlic scapes can be plain pickled or flavoured in any number of sweet or savoury pickle variations (such as sweet + tangy pickled, szechuan pickled, spicy pickled) to enjoy throughout the year. Pack in jar whole or chopped. Pickling steps, pg 80 or 81
Processing time (water bath canning):10 min

TO USE: Pickled garlic scapes are a delicious pantry treat enjoyed straight from the jar or served on charcuterie boards. Chop up and add to salads, or use them as a relish on burgers, sandwiches, or hot dogs.

KOHLRABI
—

Crisp vegetable with mellow, apple-like texture.

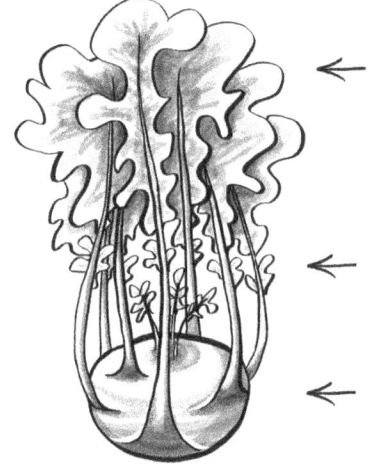

← Leaves can be cooked and eaten as you would collard greens. Try braising, adding to stir fries, sautéeing in oil until tender with salt and a squeeze of lemon juice, or cooking up with broth, onions, bacon and spices like traditional collard greens.

← Stems are woody and can be discarded.

← Root is delicious raw or cooked, tasting like a cross between an apple and a broccoli stem. After stripping the stems, peel away the tough outer skin with a vegetable peeler and cut out the circular bottom core. The flesh can be sliced and eaten raw like an apple, diced into salads or coleslaws, roasted, steamed, added to soups, or mashed.

FRESH STORAGE — Remove leafy stems from the bulb (they draw moisture away from it). Store leaves and bulb separately in sealed bags or containers in refrigerator. Leaves will last a week, bulb lasts for many weeks.

QUICK TIP — Kohlrabi pairs well with pork, chicken, and seafood, as well as ingredients like citrus, apples, fresh herbs (dill, cilantro, mint), carrots, cauliflower, beets, brussel sprouts, fennel, bacon, and mild cheeses.

PRESERVATION — Freeze, dehydrate, ferment, or pickle.
(See next page for more)

Kohlrabi leaves can also be preserved through freezing, dehydrating and turning into powder for added nutrition in recipes, or cooked and frozen. Follow methods for collard greens (pg 182)

FREEZING YOUR KOHLRABI

You can freeze your kohlrabi raw, blanched, or cooked (pg 48).
Freeze it sliced, grated, or chopped, depending on your purpose.

TO USE: Can cook directly from frozen.
Frozen kohlrabi can be added to soups, stews, curries, mashes, gratin, or roasted right from frozen. Shredded kohlrabi can be made into fritters or thawed and added to slaws.

CANNING It is not recommended to pressure can kohlrabi.

DEHYDRATING YOUR KOHLRABI

Kohlrabi takes around 6-12 hours to dehydrate, depending on their thickness. Peel. Slice thinly or small dice. Dehydrating steps, pg 63

TO USE: Enjoy dehydrated kohlrabi chips as a crunchy snack, as a crouton alternative in salads, or mix with nuts, seeds, and dried fruits for a crunchy trail mix. It can also be ground into powder and used in homemade seasoning blends, as breading for meats or vegetables, or as a boost in smoothies. Dehydrated kohlrabi can be rehydrated by soaking it in warm water for 15 minutes before use or added directly to soups and stews during cooking.

FERMENTING YOUR KOHLRABI

Fermenting kohlrabi creates a probiotic-rich, tangy condiment that can be used in salads, wraps, tacos, or enjoyed on its own. Peel. Shred, slice, or dice. Fermenting steps, pg 74

TO USE: Fermented kohlrabi can be used in salads, sandwiches, tacos or burritos, or eaten as a slaw. You can combine it with other ingredients to make a fermented salsa, relish, or dip. Add it in sushi rolls, stir fries, or grain bowls.

PICKLING YOUR KOHLRABI

Kohlrabi can be plain pickled or flavoured in any number of sweet or savoury pickle variations (such as garlic pickled, curry pickled, dill pickled, spicy pickled) to enjoy throughout the year. Peel. Slice or cut into sticks. Pickling steps, pg 80 or 81
Processing time (water bath canning):10 min

TO USE: Pickled kohlrabi is a delicious pantry snack enjoyed straight from the jar, served alongside charcuterie or cheese boards, on burgers, sandwiches, in grain bowls, or for adding a delicious crunch and zing in salads.

LEEKS

Thick, bulbous stems with sweet-onion flavour.

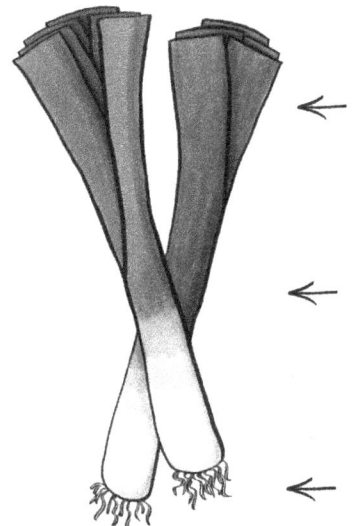

← Dark green tops are edible, though are more coarse and require longer cooking time to soften than the sweeter, lighter green parts. These are primarily used in soups and stocks, but they can also be chopped up and used in stews and casseroles.

← White and light green parts are the most tender, flavourful portion. Leeks add fragrant flavouring to things like soups, stuffings, savoury pies, or scalloped potatoes. These are also delicious fried, braised, roasted or caramelized like onions.

← Discard root portion.

FRESH STORAGE	Store unwashed and untrimmed in a sealed bag or container in refrigerator. Lasts up to 2 weeks.
QUIRKS	Leeks can be tricky to wash, as dirt often gets trapped inside their layers while growing. I recommend slicing them into pieces first (before washing) and then rinsing them in a colander to clean them more easily before cooking.
PRESERVATION	Freeze, dehydrate, ferment, or pickle. (See next page for more)

FREEZING YOUR LEEKS

You can freeze your leeks raw, blanched, or cooked (pg 48).
Freeze it chopped, ready for use. Note that freezing leeks results in a slightly softer texture once thawed, but is still a delicious addition to cooked dishes. Leeks have a strong aroma even frozen– be warned, they will smell up your whole freezer– we favour putting ours in sealed containers rather than just freezer bags to combat their aroma.

TO USE: Can cook directly from frozen.
Use frozen leeks in your soups, stews, casseroles, stuffings, gravies. Add to risotto, pilaf, omelets, quiches, frittatas, vegetable tarts, savoury pies, or savoury muffins. Or make a delicious, warming pot of potato leek soup.

CANNING It is not recommended to pressure can leeks.

DEHYDRATING YOUR LEEKS

Leeks take around 6-10 hours to dehydrate, depending on their thickness and moisture content. Slice thinly. Dehydrating steps, pg 63

TO USE: Incorporate dehydrated leeks into soups, stews, quiches, pot pies, cheesy casseroles, and baked dishes. They can add a subtle onion flavour and enhance the overall taste of dishes. Rehydrate the leeks by soaking them in warm water for a few hours or overnight before use. Stir rehydrated leeks into risotto or rice dishes, blended into creamy dips, savoury breads, or use as a pizza topping.

FERMENTING YOUR LEEKS

Fermenting leeks creates a probiotic-rich, tangy condiment that can be used in salads, sandwiches, mixed into dips and sauces, or as a topper. Fermenting steps, pg 74

TO USE: Spread fermented leeks on crostini or bruschetta for a unique and tangy appetizer (top with fresh herbs or additional toppings of your choice). Add fermented leeks to omelets, frittatas, or scrambled eggs. or use them as a topping for grilled meats. Blend fermented leeks into homemade vinaigrettes or sauces, adding depth and tanginess.

PICKLING YOUR LEEKS

Leeks can be plain pickled or flavoured in any number of pickle variations (such as mustard pickled, herb pickled, rosemary + white wine pickled) to enjoy throughout the year. Pickling steps, pg 80 or 81
Processing time (water bath canning):10 min

TO USE: Use pickled leeks as a flavorful topping for sandwiches and wraps. Toss pickled leeks into salads for a burst of flavour (works well in green salads, grain salads, or pasta salads). Mix pickled leeks into mashed potatoes or potato salads for a tangy and savoury kick. Serve alongside grilled or baked fish and seafood. Use as a topping or filling for savoury tarts and quiches. Spread pickled leeks on crostini or bruschetta for a tangy appetizer, pairing them with goat cheese or ricotta for added richness.

PAK CHOI
—

Thick, clustered stalks and leaves with tender, juicy flavour.

This entire plant is edible with thick, clustered stalks that are crunchy yet juicy, and lush green leaves having a mild, spinach-like flavour. All parts quick-cook to be beautifully tender. Commonly used in Asian cooking, the favourite ways to eat this vegetable are: braised, steamed, roasted, stir-fried, added to ramen, or served with rice or fish.

FRESH STORAGE   Store whole in a sealed bag or container in refrigerator. Lasts up to 2 weeks.

QUIRKS   All parts cook quickly, requiring only a few minutes until done. Overcooked pak choi becomes soggy and mushy. You want it tender crisp. Pan-fry it in oil for 2 minutes, steam it for 2-3 minutes, or roast (halved or quartered) for 10 minutes. Or add at the end of cooking to soups, stir fries and other recipes.

PRESERVATION   Freeze, dehydrate, ferment, or pickle.
(See next page for more)

FREEZING YOUR PAK CHOI

You can freeze your pak choi raw.
Raw freezing gives best results, blanching or cooking creates a mushy product once thawed. Freeze them chopped up, ready for use. Note that it will have a softer texture after freezing that is best used in cooked dishes.

TO USE: Can cook directly from frozen.
Frozen pak choi can be used in stir fries, soups, stews, curries, fried rice, or various Asian inspired dishes.

CANNING It is not recommended to pressure can pak choi.

DEHYDRATING YOUR PAK CHOI

Pak choi takes around 4-10 hours to dehydrate, depending on the thickness. Separate leaves from stems. Leaves can be dehydrated whole (they break apart on their own), stems should be sliced thinly. Dehydrating steps, pg 63

TO USE: Dehydrated pak choi can be rehydrated by soaking it in warm water for 15 minutes before use or added directly to soups and stews during cooking. Enjoy in noodle bowls, quiches, frittatas, or stir fries.

FERMENTING YOUR PAK CHOI

You can ferment your pak choi to use in salads, wraps, or grain bowls. Another popular way is to make kimchi, a traditional Korean fermented vegetable dish. Kimchi often includes napa cabbage, but you can use pak choi as a substitute or in combination with other vegetables. Fermenting steps, pg 74

TO USE: Make kimchi fried rice, kimchi pancakes, kimchi ramen or noodle soup, kimchi quesadillas or grilled cheese, or kimchi stir fry.

PICKLING YOUR PAK CHOI

Pak choi can be plain pickled or flavoured in any number of sweet or savoury pickle variations (such as sesame ginger pickled, mustard seed pickled, sweet and sour pickled) to enjoy throughout the year. Pickling steps, pg 80 or 81 **Processing time (water bath canning):10 min**

TO USE: Pickled pak choi can add a burst of tangy and crunchy flavour to a variety of dishes. Layer in sandwiches or wraps, as a burger topper, or chop it up and toss it in salads. Add pickled pak choi to rice bowls. noodle dishes, poke bowls, stir fries, or mix it into a dip for dumplings or spring rolls.

RHUBARB
—

Bright red stalks with tart, tangy flavour.

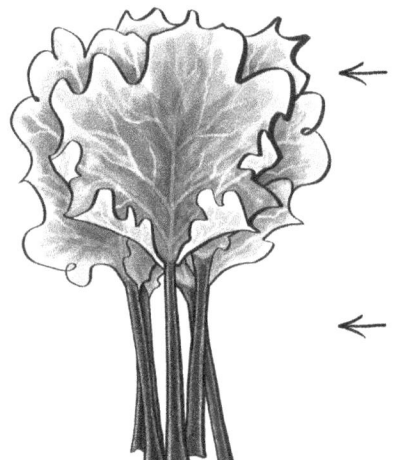

← Leaves are toxic. Discard them, do not eat them.

← Stems are very tart yet delicious when cooked or baked. Rhubarb is a vegetable often used as a fruit in desserts, pies, cakes, crumbles, jams, or muffins. Its strong, tangy flavour pairs well with the sweetness of baking, but it can also be stewed, poached, roasted, puréed, or made into a zingy BBQ sauce.

FRESH STORAGE	Chop away leaves and discard. Store unwashed stalks in a sealed bag or container in the refrigerator. Wash when ready to use. Lasts up to 3 weeks.
QUICK TIP	Rhurbarb pairs well with ingredients like **strawberries, berries, ginger, vanilla, citrus, apples, warm spices** (like cinnamon, allspice, cardamom), **coconut, pork, duck, poultry,** and **creamy cheeses**.
PRESERVATION	Freeze, pressure can, dehydrate, ferment, or pickle. (See next page for more)

FREEZING YOUR RHUBARB

You can freeze your rhubarb raw or blanched (pg 48). **I prefer raw freezing**. Freeze it chopped, ready for use.

TO USE: Can cook directly from frozen.
Use frozen rhubarb in baking (muffins, pies, cake, or crisp), or turn it into jam, sauce or compote. Spoon rhubarb compote over your morning oatmeal, cereal, or Greek yogurt for a flavorful and nutritious breakfast. Combine frozen rhubarb with other ingredients like honey, ginger, or garlic to make a savoury rhubarb sauce that pairs well with grilled or roasted meats (Rhubarb BBQ sauce). Make rhubarb syrup to add a unique twist to cocktails and mocktails, or make rhubarb sorbet.

CANNING YOUR RHUBARB

You can preserve rhubarb through **pressure canning (or water bath canning**, if sweetened). You can choose to pack the rhubarb in hot water or hot syrup. Hot water is the simpler option, but hot syrup (made with water and sugar) adds sweetness and enhances the flavour. Pressure canning steps, pg 57   **Processing time: 8 min (pints or quarts)**

DEHYDRATING YOUR RHUBARB

Rhubarb takes around 6-18 hours to dehydrate, depending on thickness and moisture content. Slice thinly. Steam until *slightly* tender (makes it taste better when rehydrated). Dehydrating steps, pg 63

TO USE: Rehydrate rhubarb by soaking it in warm water for a few hours or overnight before use. Use in recipes such as compotes, sauces, jams, baked goods, or as a flavorful addition to cereals and trail mixes. Toss rehydrated rhubarb into salads for a unique burst of flavor– it pairs well with greens, nuts, and cheese.

FERMENTING YOUR RHUBARB

Fermenting rhubarb creates a tangy and flavourful probiotic condiment that can be used in salads, sandwiches, mixed into dips and sauces, or as a side dish. Chop into desired size pieces or slice into sticks. Fermenting steps, pg 74

TO USE: Use fermented rhubarb as a condiment for grilled meats, roasted vegetables, or as a topping for burgers and sandwiches. Mix with other ingredients to create a flavourful relish or salsa. Purée fermented rhubarb and use it as a tangy spread for both cold and hot sandwiches. Serve alongside cheese and crackers as part of a cheese board. Blend fermented rhubarb with olive oil, vinegar, and herbs to create a flavorful dressing or vinaigrette for salads. Stir it into yogurt or cottage cheese for a tangy, probiotic-rich snack. Use fermented rhubarb as a unique and tangy topping for homemade pizzas. Combine it with other ingredients like cheese, caramelized onions, and prosciutto. Use it as a tangy topping for grilled fish or seafood.

PICKLING YOUR RHUBARB

Rhubarb can be plain pickled or flavoured in any number of sweet or savoury pickle variations (such as ginger + orange pickled, cardamom + vanilla pickled, maple balsamic pickled), adding delightful tanginess and crunch to a variety of dishes.
Pickling steps, pg 80 or 81   **Processing time (water bath canning):10 min**

TO USE: Spread pickled rhubarb on crostini or bruschetta for a flavorful appetizer— it works well with soft cheeses like goat cheese or cream cheese. Add it to charcuterie boards, or use as a topper for burgers, pulled pork or chicken sliders for a tangy and refreshing contrast to the savory meat. Purée pickled rhubarb to make a tangy sauce or relish and use as a topping for grilled meats or various dishes.

SCALLIONS

Long, slender greens with mild onion flavour.
(aka. Green Onions)

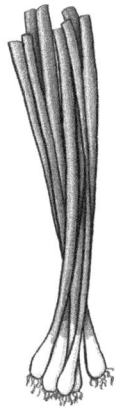

 Entire plant is edible aside from the roots. Their bright colour and mild onion flavour make them excellent for using raw. They are often found in salads, eggs, fresh salsas, noodles, omelets, tacos, or as garnish. They can also be roasted whole with a drizzle of olive oil and sprinkle of salt or added to your stir fries.

Discard root portion.

FRESH STORAGE	Providing your green onions still have their roots, the best way to store them is upright in a jar with enough cold water in the bottom to cover their base (about an inch). Next, place a plastic bag over the entire thing and store it in the refrigerator. Refill water as necessary. (Alternatively, you can keep them in a sealed plastic bag or container in the refrigerator.) Lasts up to 3 weeks.
QUICK TIP	Scallions can easily be added to just about anything. They pair particularly well with ingredients like garlic, lime, soy sauce, ginger, sesame oil, cilantro, chicken, fish, and mild cheeses. They work well in any dish where raw onion would be too strong.
PRESERVATION	Freeze, dehydrate, ferment, or pickle. (See next page for more)

FREEZING YOUR SCALLIONS

You can freeze your scallions raw or blanched (pg 48).
I recommend raw freezing. Freeze them whole or chopped, ready for use. Note that freezing scallions result in a slightly softer texture once thawed, but they are still a delicious addition to cooked dishes.

TO USE: Can cook directly from frozen.
Use frozen scallions in your soups, stews, casseroles, stuffings, gravies. Add to risotto, pilaf, fried rice, omelets, quiches, frittatas, vegetable tarts, savoury pies, or savoury muffins.

CANNING It is not recommended to pressure can scallions.

DEHYDRATING YOUR SCALLIONS

Scallions take around 3-8 hours to dehydrate. Chop into small pieces. Separate out the denser, whiter pieces (these will take longer to dry). Dehydrating steps, pg 63

TO USE: Dehydrated scallions can be used in soups, stews, casseroles, sauces, and many other dishes. They provide a concentrated flavour, and their long shelf life makes them a convenient pantry staple. Add to bread dough, savoury muffins or scones. Sprinkle over mashed or scalloped potatoes or use as a garnish for soups or grilled meats.

FERMENTING YOUR SCALLIONS

Fermenting scallions creates a probiotic-rich, tangy topping for salads, sandwiches, and various dishes. Ferment whole (to chop later) or chopped. Fermenting steps, pg 74

TO USE: Fermented scallions can be added to grain bowls, broths, egg dishes or incorporated into sourdough bread. Blend them into sour cream or yogurt-based dips to add depth and a tangy kick. Sprinkle fermented scallions on baked or mashed potatoes.

PICKLING YOUR SCALLIONS

Scallions can be plain pickled or flavoured in any number of sweet or savoury pickle variations to enjoy throughout the year. Pickling steps, pg 80 or 81   **Processing time (water bath canning):10 min**

TO USE: Pickled scallions can add a tangy kick to your tacos or burritos or as a topper to grilled chicken, fish, or beef. Sprinkle over salads to add a burst of flavour, particularly those with Asian or Mexican-inspired dressings. Layer pickled scallions onto sandwiches or wraps for a zesty twist-- they can add brightness to both cold and hot sandwiches. Use as a garnish or topper for deviled eggs, scrambled eggs, omelets and frittatas, or blend into salad dressings, aioli, or dipping sauces for an extra layer of complexity.

LEAVES

Vegetables // grown for their leaves

ARUGULA
—

Wispy leafy green with peppery, slightly tart flavour.

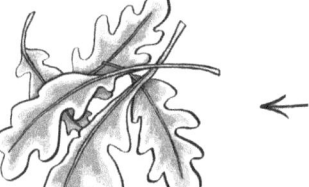

Leaves are most commonly enjoyed raw but can also be sautéed. Turn up the flavour in your salads, sandwiches, pizzas, rice bowls, sheet pan suppers, or pasta by adding this bold, leafy green as a generous garnish or a base. It can be added during the final moments of cooking for a slight softening or blitzed into a delicious pesto (pg 39).

FRESH STORAGE — Store leaves in a sealed bag in the refrigerator. Rinse and pat dry (or use a salad spinner) before use. Leaves last a week.

QUICK TIP — Arugula pairs well with ingredients like beets, radishes, pickled onions, citrus, balsamic, other vinegars, sweet fruits (berries, apple, pear), dried fruits, nuts, sharp or tangy cheeses (blue cheese, goat cheese, feta), roasted red peppers, sundried tomatoes, and prosciutto. Its bold flavour makes a great match with other strong flavours.

PRESERVATION — Freeze in oil, dehydrate and turn into flakes for added nutrition and flavour in recipes, or make into pesto (pg 39) and freeze. (See next page for more)

FREEZING YOUR ARUGULA

The best way to freeze arugula is to freeze it in oil. Regular freezing will lead to a wilted or mushy texture when thawed. Freezing arugula in oil will alter the texture somewhat, so it will be best used in cooked or blended dishes rather than fresh salads. **To freeze:** Simply coat the arugula in a layer of olive oil or other neutral oil. Divide into portions suitable for your needs and place in small containers or zip-top bags. Freeze.

TO USE: Can cook directly from frozen.
Toss frozen arugula into pasta dishes during the last few minutes of cooking. It also works well in both creamy and tomato-based sauces. Add to sautéed vegetables or make into arugula pesto. Incorporate into omelets, frittatas, or scrambled eggs. Use it as a pizza topping, or add a handful to your grilled cheese sandwich or panini for a peppery kick.

DEHYDRATING YOUR ARUGULA

Arugula takes around 4-8 hours to dehydrate. Leaves can be dehydrated whole (they break apart on their own once dry). Dehydrating steps, pg 63

TO USE: Dehydrated arugula is a versátile ingredient that can add a peppery flavour to various recipes. Crumble dehydrated arugula directly into dishes like soups, stews, salads, or sauces. Sprinkle on top of pizzas before baking, the heat of the oven will help release its flavors. Grind it into a powder and use it as a seasoning or herb blend. Incorporate into bread or savory baked goods like focaccia, savory muffins, or crackers for a distinctive flavor.

Dehydrated arugula can be more potent than fresh, so start with a smaller amount and adjust to your taste.

COLLARD GREENS
—

Hearty leafy green with subtle earthy flavour.

← Leaves are hearty and very nutritious. They are often braised, creamed, or stewed with meats as they can withstand longer cooking times. Commonly sautéed with caramelized onions and bacon, they can also be sautéed with a bit of oil, garlic, and a drizzle of lemon, steamed, or even chopped up raw in salads. The flavour is a cross between cabbage and hearty kale.

← Stems are woody and tough. Remove and discard.

FRESH STORAGE	Store in a sealed bag without washing (I recommend removing and discarding stems first). Leaves are large, so don't be afraid to pack as much as you can into the bag. Push the air out of the bag before sealing. Store in refrigerator until use. Rinse or wash before using. Leaves last a week.
QUICK TIP	Collard greens pair wonderfully with meats, including ham, ribs, bacon, pulled pork, sausage, roast beef, fried chicken, and catfish. Other complimentary items are baked beans, green beans, rice, potatoes, and sweet potatoes. Collard greens are a common staple in southern cooking.
PRESERVATION	Freeze, pressure can, dehydrate, ferment, or pickle. (See next page for more)

FREEZING YOUR COLLARD GREENS

You can freeze your collard greens raw, blanched, or cooked (pg 48). Remove tough stems and discard. Freeze greens chopped, ready for use.

TO USE: Can cook directly from frozen.
Use frozen collard greens in your soups, stews, casseroles, stuffings, and gravies. Add to rice dishes, quiches, frittatas or as a filling for wraps and burritos. Sauté them with garlic, onions, and your favourite seasonings for a nutritious side.

CANNING YOUR COLLARD GREENS

You can preserve raw collard greens through **pressure canning** for use in soups, stews, casseroles, or as a side. Discard stems and loosely chop leaves. Pressure canning steps, pg 57 **Processing time: 75 min (pints) 90 min (quarts)**

DEHYDRATING YOUR COLLARD GREENS

Collard greens take around 6-10 hours to dehydrate. Remove tough stems and discard. Chop or slice leaves as desired. Blanch for 2 minutes. Dehydrating steps, pg 63

TO USE: Enjoy dehydrated collard greens as a crunchy snack, or sprinkle them over grain or rice bowls for added texture and nutritional boost. Mix dehydrated greens into casseroles or baked pasta dishes; drying concentrates their flavour, making them a delicious addition. Grind dehydrated collard greens into a powder to add to your smoothies for extra nutrition. Rehydrate the greens by soaking them in hot water for about 20-30 minutes and use them in sautés or stir-fries.

FERMENTING YOUR COLLARD GREENS

Fermented collard greens add a probiotic-rich, tangy flavour to various dishes. Remove tough stems. Keep leaves whole or chop them into pieces. Fermenting steps, pg 74

TO USE: Use large, fermented collard green leaves as wraps for your favourite fillings, such as veggies, grains, and proteins. The tangy flavour adds a delightful twist. Chop fermented collard greens and add them to salads for a burst of flavour and a probiotic boost. Blend fermented collard greens with yogurt or cream cheese to create a tangy dip perfect for veggies or crackers. Add to scrambled eggs or omelets or in soups for a tangy and nutritious element (stir them in just before serving to retain the probiotic benefits).

PICKLING YOUR COLLARD GREENS

Collard greens can be plain pickled or flavoured in any number of sweet or savoury pickle variations (such as soy ginger pickled, maple balsamic pickled, olive + herb pickled) to enjoy throughout the year. Pickling steps, pg 80 or 81
Processing time (water bath canning):10 min

TO USE: Pickled collard greens make a tasty topper for pulled pork, rice or noodle bowls, or eggs. They can be served alongside grilled meats or vegetables. The tangy flavour balances the richness of BBQ or grilled meats.

HERBS
—

Leaves used for their fragrant and aromatic qualities.

Fresh herbs are a flavour and freshness powerhouse to add to your cooking, in addition to being nutritious. Strip leaves from stem, discard stems. Chopping up the leaves breaks open the cells, releasing their fragrant aromas.

Soft herbs (basil, dill, parsley, chives, cilantro) are delicious raw, usually chopped or chiffonade, and added to salads or scattered over/stirred into already cooked food.

Woody-stemmed herbs (e.g. rosemary, thyme) are tougher, with an overpowering raw flavour, so are usually cooked.

FRESH STORAGE — Loosely roll fresh herbs in a damp paper towel and place in a sealed bag or container in the refrigerator. Last between 2-3 weeks.

QUICK TIP — With your soft herbs (see next page), if your bunch is drying out or going limp, they can be reinvigorated by trimming 1/4" off the bottom and placed in a jar of cold water for a few hours to overnight in the refrigerator. Once it is good as new, return to sealed bag or container.

PRESERVATION — Freeze in oil, or dehydrate and grind into flakes or powder.
(See next page for more)

Types of Herbs

There are thousands of different herbs around the world, each with its own unique qualities. Some are used for culinary purposes, others for medicinal purposes, aromatic purposes, and teas. Fresh culinary herbs add delicious depth of flavour to cooking and fall into these two categories:

Soft Herbs — Tender and delicate in texture. These are best enjoyed raw. Add to salads, sprinkle over food, or stir into recipes at the end of cooking. Includes:
Basil, dill, parsley, chives, mint, cilantro, tarragon, chervil, sorrel

Hard Herbs — Tough and woody in texture, with flavours too powerful to be eaten raw. These are best cooked, added at the beginning of recipes to infuse flavour. You can chop them (stems removed) or add them whole and remove before serving. Includes:
Rosemary, thyme, savory, oregano, marjoram, sage, bay leaves

NOTE: These categories are not strict. Some herbs can fit into both groups. Personal preferences and regional traditions influence how herbs are used in cooking.

FREEZING YOUR HERBS

Freeze fresh herbs in oil. Freezing herbs in oil retain their aromatic qualities and concentrated flavour.

To freeze: Divide chopped herbs or whole leaves into ice cube trays or small containers. Pour enough olive oil or neutral oil into each compartment to cover the herbs. Place in the freezer and allow to freeze completely; this may take a few hours. Once frozen, remove them from the trays or containers and transfer to freezer-safe bags (remember to label for easy identification later).

TO USE: When ready to use the herbs, simply grab the desired number of cubes and add them directly to your cooking. The oil will melt, releasing the herbs into your dish.

DRYING YOUR HERBS

To dry your herbs, use a dehydrator or hang them in tied bunches upside down (pg 63). It can take anywhere from a few days to a couple of weeks to fully dry, depending on the type of herb, humidity, and temperature. Check regularly to prevent over-drying. They are ready when the leaves crumble easily between your fingers. Once fully dried, grind the leaves into flakes or powder and store in sealed bags, jars, or containers to use at your leisure. Lasts up to 3 years.

ENDIVE
—

Light cylindrical heads with bitter, cup-shaped leaves.

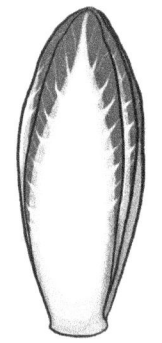

 Entire plant is edible and can be eaten raw or cooked. With their crisp texture and refined look, leaves are often separated and served raw for use in appetizers, with dips in place of crackers, or for added elegance in salads. When cooked, their bitter flavour mellows and becomes nutty. Braise, bake, or roast them whole or halved.

 If cooking whole, you can carefully nip off the base so the head still holds together. If separating the leaves, slice off and discard the base.

FRESH STORAGE — Store in a tightly sealed bag or container without washing. Store in refrigerator until use. Rinse or wash just before using. Lasts a week.

QUICK TIP — Endive pairs well with ingredients like walnuts, pears, vinegars, citrus, fennel, parsley, chives, dijon, spicy greens like arugula and radicchio, and strong or sharp cheeses (parmesan, goat cheese, blue cheese).

To crisp up leaves for use, submerge them in a bowl of ice water for 10-15 minutes, then pat dry. Return to refrigerator until ready to use.

PRESERVATION — Ferment, pickle.
(See next page for more)

FREEZING It is not recommended to freeze endive, it will be very mushy when thawed.

CANNING It is not recommended to pressure can endive.

FERMENTING YOUR ENDIVE

Fermenting endive is not common, but it can be done. Fermenting steps, pg 74
Use in similar ways to other fermented vegetables.

PICKLING YOUR ENDIVE

Endives can be plain pickled or flavoured in any number of pickle variations (such as garlic + herb pickled, turmeric pickled, fennel + orange pickled) to enjoy throughout the year. Pickling steps, pg 80 or 81   **Processing time (water bath canning):10 min**

TO USE: Toss pickled endive into green or grain salads for an extra layer of flavour and crunch. Use as a flavorful addition to charcuterie boards or appetizer platters, pair it with cheeses, cured meats, and olives. Spread goat cheese or cream cheese on crostini and top with pickled endive for an elegant and flavorful appetizer. Float pickled endive on top of soups or stews just before serving, adding a bright and tangy note to the dish.

KALE

—

Sturdy leafy green with mild, earthy flavour.

← Leaves can be eaten raw or cooked and boast many health benefits. Kale leaves can be sautéed, grilled, added to soups, tenderized, made into pesto (pg 39) or kale chips, added raw to salads, or cooked into your favourite dish. They lend themselves well to any dish calling for greens, as well as being a popular ingredient in juices or smoothies.

← Stems are woody and can be discarded.

FRESH STORAGE	Store leaves in a sealed bag without washing (remove stems first if desired). Leaves are large; don't be afraid to pack as much as you can into the bag. Push the air out of the bag before sealing. Store in refrigerator until use. Rinse or wash before using. Leaves last a week.
QUIRKS	Kale leaves can be quite fibrous when eaten raw compared to other greens unless massaged first. Massaging kale with a bit of oil and lemon juice will make it tender, flavourful, and pleasant for your salads and grain bowls.
	HOW TO: Place chopped kale in a bowl, add a squeeze of lemon juice and a drizzle of olive oil. Using your hands, massage leaves for 2 minutes to coat and soften them. Kale will look glossy. Add a pinch of salt for extra flavour.
PRESERVATION	Freeze, pressure can, dehydrate, ferment, or pickle. (See next page for more)

FREEZING YOUR KALE

You can freeze your kale raw, blanched, or cooked (pg 48).
Remove tough stems and discard. Freeze leaves torn or chopped, ready for use.
I recommend just freezing raw, packed tight in sealable freezer bags with as much air as possible squeezed out.

TO USE: Can cook directly from frozen.
Frozen kale is a convenient and nutritious ingredient to have on hand. Add to lasagna, baked pasta dishes, soups and stews. Top grain bowls or Buddha bowls with thawed or lightly sautéed frozen kale. Use as a pizza topping, add to smoothies, or use in stir fries.

CANNING YOUR KALE

You can preserve kale through **pressure canning** for use in your favourite recipes or as a side dish. The canning process softens it up, making the leaves tasty and tender. Discard stems and loosely chop leaves. Pressure canning steps, pg 57
Processing time: 70 min (pints) 90 min (quarts)

DEHYDRATING YOUR KALE

Kale takes around 3-6 hours to dehydrate. Remove stalks and discard. Leaves can be dehydrated whole (they break apart once dry). Dehydrating steps, pg 63

TO USE: Enjoy dehydrated kale chips as a crunchy snack. Experiment with different seasonings to create unique flavours for your kale chips. Crumble dehydrated kale into soups and stews for a quick and nutritious boost. It rehydrates during cooking and adds a lovely texture. Grind it into powder and mix with herbs and spices to create a homemade seasoning blend for roasted vegetables, meats, or popcorn. Rehydrate kale by soaking it in warm water for 10-15 minutes and adding it to pastas, grain dishes or casseroles.

FERMENTING YOUR KALE

Fermenting kale creates a probiotic-rich, tangy addition to salads, sandwiches, pasta, or as a side dish. Fermented kale can also involve making a type of sauerkraut or kimchi. Discard stems and loosely chop leaves. Fermenting steps, pg 74

TO USE: Add fermented kale to sandwiches or wraps for a unique and probiotic-rich layer. Use as a topping for homemade pizzas or flatbreads. Add to omelets, frittatas, scrambled eggs, grain bowls or buddha bowls. Toss into salads for an extra burst of flavour and probiotics, or add to your fruit smoothies.

PICKLING YOUR KALE

Kale can be plain pickled or flavoured in any number of pickle variations (such as spicy pickled, miso pickled, smoky pickled) to enjoy throughout the year. Pickling steps, pg 80 or 81
Processing time (water bath canning):10 min

TO USE: Add pickled kale to sandwiches or wraps for a zesty and crunchy element. It pairs well with deli meats, cheese, and condiments. Use in tacos or burritos for a refreshing and tangy contrast to savoury fillings. Layer pickled kale into grilled cheese sandwiches or paninis, or use it as a pizza topping. It can provide a tangy contrast to the richness of cheese and other toppings. Incorporate into grain or pasta salads or add to quinoa or couscous bowls. Add savoury pies, quiches, or turnovers for an added layer of flavour.

LETTUCE
—

Loosely packed head with mild, refreshing leaves.

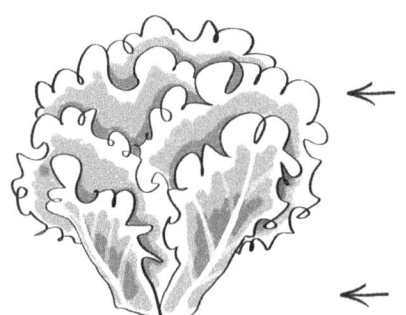

← Leaves are almost exclusively eaten raw as the primary base for salads or a fresh topper for sandwiches, wraps, and burgers. Different lettuce varieties offer varying levels of crunch, texture, and bitterness. Separate leaves and rinse/wash well before using.

← Discard the base.

FRESH STORAGE	Store in the refrigerator. First, remove any damaged or wilted leaves. Moisture is the enemy of lettuce, so wrap the lettuce head in a paper towel (or a clean dish towel) and store it in a sealed plastic bag. Before use, rinse the leaves and dry them using a salad spinner (or pat dry with a clean towel). Lettuce lasts a week.
	Alternatively, chop up your lettuce into pieces, rinse, and dry it with a salad spinner. Put pieces in a sealed bag or container and top with a clean folded wash cloth or paper towel to absorb excess moisture (change this out every few days). Lasts 2 weeks.
QUIRKS	If your lettuce is limp or wilting, you can crisp it up by submerging leaves in a bowl of ice water for 10-15 minutes, then patting dry. Return to the refrigerator until use.
PRESERVATION	There is no great way to preserve lettuce. All methods end up with a limp, wilted, or mushy product. Best to enjoy that lettuce fresh!

RADICCHIO
—

Cabbage-like, leafy head with spicy, bitter flavour.

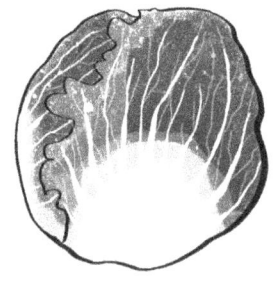 Entire plant is edible and known for its spicy bitterness. It can be eaten raw or cooked. With crisp texture and beautiful appearance, these leaves are often chopped or shredded for use salads, slaws, or appetizers. When cooked, its bitter flavour mellows. Roast, bake, sauté, or grill in wedges, or add to cooked recipes.

 Discard the base.

FRESH STORAGE	Store in a tightly sealed bag or container without washing. Store in refrigerator until use. Rinse or wash just before using. Lasts a week.
QUICK TIP	Radicchio pairs well with ingredients like beets, fennel, citrus, vinegars, pear, bacon, butternut squash, arugula, basil, nuts, and stronger cheeses (gorgonzola, feta).
PRESERVATION	Dehydrate, ferment, pickle. (See next page for more) *Fermented or pickled makes radicchio taste even better!*

FREEZING It is not recommended to freeze radicchio, it will be mushy when thawed.

CANNING It is not recommended to pressure can radicchio.

DEHYDRATING YOUR RADICCHIO

Radicchio takes around 4-6 hours to dehydrate. Cut leaves into strips or bite-size pieces. Dehydrating steps, pg 63

TO USE: Note that the intensity of radicchio's flavour is concentrated when dehydrated, so a little goes a long way. Experiment with small amounts at first to determine your preferred level of flavour in different dishes.

Sprinkle dehydrated radicchio over grain bowls for added crunch and flavour. It pairs well with quinoa, rice, or couscous. Incorporate dehydrated radicchio into casseroles, soups, or stews. The cooking process will rehydrate the radicchio, infusing the dish with its distinct taste. Rehydrate radicchio by soaking it in warm water for 10-20 minutes and use it in salads to add a burst of flavour and a slightly chewy texture.

FERMENTING YOUR RADICCHIO

Fermented radicchio adds a tangy and complex flavour to dishes. Keep leaves whole, or cut into strips or bite-size pieces. Fermenting steps, pg 74

TO USE: Toss into salads for a burst of tanginess. It pairs well with other greens, fruits, nuts, and cheese. Incorporate it into grain bowls (using quinoa or farro) for added depth of flavour. Include fermented radicchio on charcuterie or cheese boards. Its tangy taste can balance the richness of cheeses and cured meats.

PICKLING YOUR RADICCHIO

Radicchio can be plain pickled or flavoured in any number of pickle variations (such as balsamic pickled, honey mustard pickled, curry pickled) to enjoy throughout the year. Keep leaves whole, or cut into strips or bite-size pieces. Pickling steps, pg 80 or 81
Processing time (water bath canning):10 min

TO USE: Serve pickled radicchio as a side on meat and cheese platters or charcuterie boards. Use as a topping for burgers and sliders, tacos and tostadas, or grain bowls. Toss pickled radicchio into salads to add a burst of tanginess. It pairs well with other salad greens, nuts, fruits, and cheeses.

SPINACH
—

Springy leaves with mild, herby flavour.

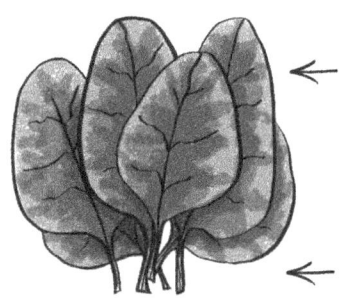

← These leaves are nutrient-dense and very versatile to consume. They can be eaten raw in salads, sandwiches or wraps, and are wonderful cooked and incorporated into recipes. They are delicious with eggs (think quiches, omelettes, or frittatas) and as a standalone side (think sautéed spinach or creamed spinach). They also pack a nutritional punch in juices or smoothies.

← Stems are not as tender as the leaves but can still be cooked and consumed. The stems of mature spinach can be tough and fibrous compared to those of young or baby spinach (which is more enjoyable to eat). Some people prefer to trim the stems before cooking.

FRESH STORAGE — Store unwashed leaves in refrigerator in a sealed plastic bag. Remove any damaged or wilted leaves first. Moisture is the enemy of spinach, so place a folded paper towel inside the bag to absorb any excess moisture. Before use, rinse leaves and use a salad spinner to dry (or pat dry with a clean towel). Lasts 5 days.

QUIRKS — When eaten raw, spinach can cause a gritty or chalky feeling on your teeth. This harmless sensation is caused by the oxalic acid in the spinach reacting to the calcium in your teeth. You can solve this by squeezing lemon juice over the leaves and tossing them, or by blanching/cooking them to dissolve the acid if desired.

PRESERVATION — Freeze, Dehydrate, Pickle
(See next page for more)

FREEZING YOUR SPINACH

You can freeze your spinach raw, blanched, or cooked (pg 48).
Freeze it whole or chopped. You may prefer to remove the stems first and freeze only the tender leaves, depending on your preference.

TO USE: Can use directly from frozen or **thaw frozen spinach and drain excess moisture before using it in recipes to prevent the dish from becoming too watery.** Add into casseroles such as lasagna, baked ziti, or spinach and feta stuffed chicken. Add to omelettes or quiches, or pasta dishes (like spaghetti, Alfredo, macaroni, and cheese). Toss frozen spinach into soups and stews during the last few minutes of cooking. Blend thawed, well-drained spinach into dips like spinach and artichoke dip, add to bread or muffin batter for a savoury twist or use as a filling for traditional Greek spanakopita (spinach pie) or other pastries.

CANNING It is not recommended to pressure can spinach.

DEHYDRATING YOUR SPINACH

Spinach takes around 3-8 hours to dehydrate. Trim off any tough stems. Dehydrating steps, pg 63

TO USE: Add dehydrated spinach to soups, stews, and broths. Add crushed dehydrated spinach to bread or savoury muffin batter. Grind it into a powder and use it as a seasoning-- add it to homemade spice blends and sauces or sprinkle it over popcorn. Incorporate it into homemade snack mixes with nuts, seeds, and dried fruits. Rehydrate spinach by soaking it in warm water for a few minutes until it is pliable. Add rehydrated spinach to lasagnas or other casseroles, soups and stews, pasta, rice dishes, omelets or scrambled eggs, dips and spreads, or use it as a pizza topping.

FERMENTING YOUR SPINACH

Fermenting spinach is not common practice. It is challenging to ferment successfully due to its higher water content. Use in similar ways to other fermented vegetables.

PICKLING YOUR SPINACH

Spinach is not traditionally pickled like cucumbers or other firm vegetables. However, you can create a quick-pickled spinach dish by marinating it in a vinegar-based brine. This method doesn't involve any fermentation but imparts a tangy flavour to the spinach. It must be stored in the refrigerator and consumed within a relatively short period, typically a few weeks. Adjust the quantities of sugar, salt, and vinegar to suit your preferences.

TO USE: Serve marinated spinach as a tangy side dish or as an addition to salads, sandwiches, wraps, burgers, tacos, or grain bowls.

SWISS CHARD

Mild, pleasant, leafy green with crisp, juicy stalks.

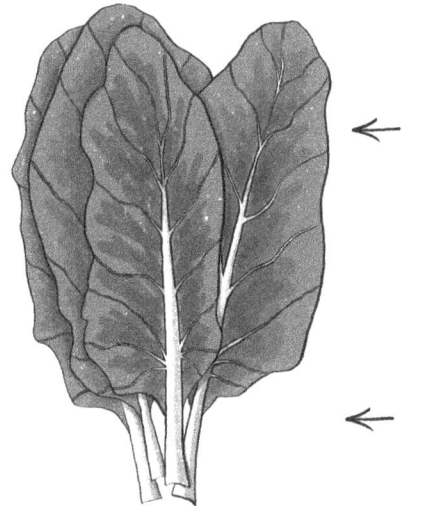

← Leaves are tender and delicious. Strip greens from stems for a wonderful substitute for spinach or other greens in recipes. They are delicious braised, sautéed with onions and garlic, cooked with eggs, and are suitable for eating raw in sandwiches or salads.

← Stalks are also delicious and nutritious, with a slight celery-like flavour. They take longer to cook than the leaves, so they are often stripped and cooked before adding the leaves. They can also be pickled (pg 80 or 81), added to stir fries, baked into gratins, or added to soups.

FRESH STORAGE — Rinse briefly and lightly shake dry. Swiss Chard does better with a bit of moisture to revive it, but it should not be sopping wet. Pat dry and place in a sealed bag or container in the refrigerator. Lasts 1-2 weeks.

QUICK TIP — Swiss chard pairs well with any roasted or grilled meats, as well as ingredients like garlic, lemon, vinegar, bacon, nuts, parmesan, white beans, and coconut milk.

PRESERVATION — Freeze, dehydrate, ferment, or pickle.
(See next page for more)

FREEZING YOUR SWISS CHARD

You can freeze your chard raw, blanched, or cooked (pg 48).
You may prefer to freeze leaves and stems separately. Freeze chopped or whole (with leaves rolled up for easy frozen chopping later). **I recommend freezing raw** in sealable freezer bags with as much air as possible squeezed out. Note that the texture does change once thawed (it becomes somewhat limp), so it is best used for cooked dishes.

TO USE: Can cook directly from frozen.
Add frozen swiss chard to chili, lasagna, baked pasta dishes, gratin, stews, or hearty winter soups. It pairs well with eggs. Mix thawed and drained chard into quiche or frittata fillings. Sauté or steam frozen swiss chard and serve it as a side dish, seasoned with garlic, olive oil, and a squeeze of lemon.

CANNING It is not recommended to pressure can swiss chard.

DEHYDRATING YOUR SWISS CHARD

Swiss chard takes around 3-10 hours to dehydrate. Separate leaves from stems before drying. Slice stems thinly. Dehydrating steps, pg 63

TO USE: Rehydrate swiss chard by soaking the leaves in water for a few minutes until they become pliable. Add rehydrated chard to lasagnas or other casseroles, soups and stews, rice dishes, in omelets or scrambled eggs, or use as a pizza topping.

FERMENTING YOUR SWISS CHARD

Fermenting swiss chard creates a probiotic-rich, tangy condiment that can be used in salads and sandwiches, mixed into dips, or eaten as a side dish. Separate leaves from stems, or leave whole, as desired. Chop stems into bite-sized pieces. Fermenting steps, pg 74

TO USE: Toss fermented swiss chard into salads for an extra burst of flavor and a probiotic boost. Use as a tasty filling for wraps or sandwiches. Add to buddha bowls or rice dishes, or blend it into sauces or salad dressings for a unique twist. You can also add a small amount of fermented swiss chard to your smoothies for a tangy and probiotic boost.

PICKLING YOUR SWISS CHARD

Swiss chard can be plain pickled or flavoured with additions such as garlic cloves, peppercorns, mustard seeds, dill, or other pickling spices. Separate leaves from stems if desired. Many folks pickle just the colourful stalks (in chopped pieces or as sticks). Pickling steps, pg 80 or 81
Processing time (water bath canning):10 min

TO USE: Add pickled swiss chard to your favorite salads for a tangy kick. Use it as a zesty topping for sandwiches and wraps, or incorporate it into tacos or burritos. Serve pickled chard as a tasty side dish alongside grilled meats, fish, or vegetarian main courses. Roll it into summer rolls or sushi for a unique and tangy twist, use it as a flavorful garnish for soups and stews, or as a topper for rice bowls.

MICROGREENS

Young seedlings of vegetables and herbs in a variety of flavours.

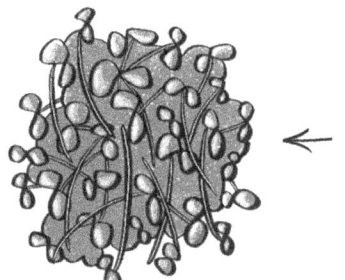

These tender, delicious sprouts come in many varieties with all sorts of intense and unique flavours. They are visually pleasing and can be used as a tasty topper for just about anything. Add raw to salads, burgers, wraps, sandwiches, and rice bowls, use to brighten up a pasta dish, or rest them delicately over eggs.

FRESH STORAGE | Store in a sealed bag or container in refrigerator. Lasts a week.

QUIRKS | Microgreens are simply the young seedlings of vegetables and herbs, but they pack a nutritional punch! They contain concentrated levels of the nutrients (and flavours) found in the mature adult vegetable, so whenever you add these to your meal, you are getting a healthy, delicious boost and not just a pretty plate.

PRESERVATION | There is no great way to preserve microgreens. All methods end up with a limp, wilted, or mushy product. Best to enjoy those babies fresh!

BULBS

Vegetables // grown for their bulb

GARLIC

Edible bulb clusters with intense aromatic flavour.

 ← Garlic cloves are enjoyed both raw and cooked. Raw adds a punchy kick to dressings and dips, and sautéed or cooked adds a mellow aromatic flavour to recipes. Loosen the bulb to separate the cloves. Trim the bottoms and peel away the papery skin to access the flavourful, edible clove. Mince, chop, or slice for use in cooking, or roast the head whole drizzled with oil.

FRESH STORAGE Store whole heads at room temperature in a dry place with plenty of air circulation. A basket or garlic holder on your counter (out of the sun) works well. Lasts for months.

QUICK TIP Roasting whole garlic makes it creamy and spreadable, creating a mellow, nutty, rich flavour that can be added to recipes.

HOW TO: Preheat oven to 400°. Trim 1/4" off the top of each head of garlic, exposing the cloves. Place, cut side up, on a piece of aluminum foil. Drizzle with olive oil. Wrap the heads up with the foil and place in a small ramekin, muffin tin, or baking dish. Bake for 30-45 minutes or until cloves are golden, caramelized, and soft when pressed. Once cool, the cloves will easily squeeze out.

PRESERVATION Freeze, dehydrate, ferment, or pickle.
(See next page for more)

FREEZING YOUR GARLIC

You can freeze your garlic raw or in oil.
Freeze them chopped, minced, or in whole peeled cloves. I prefer peeled whole cloves (easy to grab and chop as needed for any dish) or minced in ice cube trays with a bit of oil over the top (portioned for easy sautéeing and cooking). Transfer cubes to a sealable freezer bag once frozen.

TO USE: Can cook directly from frozen. Use as you would fresh garlic.

CANNING It is not recommended to pressure can garlic.

DEHYDRATING YOUR GARLIC

Garlic takes around 4-8 hours to dehydrate, depending on the thickness of the slices. Peel and discard base. Slice thinly. Dehydrating steps, pg 63

TO USE: You can add dehydrated garlic directly to soups, stews, sauces, or other recipes that involve cooking with liquids, or you can rehydrate it by soaking it in warm water for 15 minutes. Grind it into powder and use it for seasoning (pg 67), spice rubs, and marinades. Mix dehydrated garlic into bread dough or other baked goods for a savoury twist (the moisture in the dough will rehydrate the garlic as the bread bakes).

When using dehydrated garlic, keep in mind that it is more potent than fresh garlic, so you may need to adjust the quantity based on your taste preferences. Experiment with small amounts initially and add more if needed.

FERMENTING YOUR GARLIC

Fermented garlic has a unique, tangy flavour and a softer texture compared to fresh garlic. Use it to add depth and complexity to your dishes. Peel and discard base. Leave whole or slice thinly. Or blitz it with salt in a food processor to make delicious fermented garlic paste. Fermenting steps, pg 74

TO USE: Mash fermented garlic and spread it on toasted bread or crackers for a flavorful and tangy garlic spread. Incorporate it into dips (like hummus, tzatziki, and guacamole) or blend it into pasta sauces, salad dressings, or marinades. Add to soups, stews, and chili, or use as a pizza topping. Make a fermented garlic aioli (blend with mayonnaise) as a dip or condiment for sandwiches, roasted potato wedges, and seafood.

PICKLING YOUR GARLIC

Garlic can be plain pickled or flavoured in any number of sweet or savoury pickle variations (such as lemon pepper pickled, smoky pickled) to use throughout the year. Peel whole cloves and fill jar. Pickling steps, pg 80 or 81
Processing time (water bath canning):10 min

TO USE: Blend pickled garlic into softened butter to create a flavorful spread for bread or finishing touch for cooked dishes. Chop pickled garlic and mix it into sauces, whether for pasta, seafood, or dipping for a unique flavor element. Serve pickled garlic as a condiment for grilled meats, its tangy flavor complements the richness of the dishes. Or serve as part of an antipasto platter with olives, cheese, cured meats, and crusty bread.

ONIONS
—

Edible bulb of concentric layers with potent flavour.

Onions are enjoyed both raw and cooked. Use raw in salads, sandwiches, burgers, tacos, and fresh salsas. Raw onions add an aromatic punch to recipes, whereas sautéeing or cooking onions mellows and sweetens their flavour. Trim ends and peel away the papery skin to access the flavourful, edible center. Slice or chop for use in cooking, grilling, marinating, or pickling.

Green tops are also edible. Fresh summer onions come with their green tops still attached. Green onion tops add fragrant flavouring to things like soups, stuffings, savoury pies, or scalloped potatoes. They are delicious fried, braised, roasted, or caramelized.

FRESH STORAGE — Onions with green tops still attached are fresh onions (not yet cured). These should be stored in the refrigerator in a sealed bag or container. Onions with a hardy, dry outer skin have been cured. Store them in a cool, dry, dark place rather than the refrigerator, such as the pantry, back of a cupboard, or the garage. Do not store in plastic bags (unless they have holes for ventilation), rather use paper bags, baskets, or buckets without lids so the air can circulate around them. Do not store onions directly next to your other storage items, as they can cause premature spoilage.

QUIRKS — Cutting onions produces a chemical irritant that stings the eyes and prompts tears. There are a few ways to prevent crying or at least slow it down. Breathe through your mouth (not your nose) while cutting, or try chilling your onions in the refrigerator for 24 hours (or a 30-minute blast in the freezer) beforehand.

PRESERVATION — Freeze, dehydrate, ferment, or pickle.
(See next page for more)

Green onion tops can be preserved similar to scallions (pg 172).

FREEZING YOUR ONIONS

You can freeze your onions raw, blanched, or cooked (pg 48).
Freeze them peeled and chopped, sliced, or whole depending on your purpose. I **recommend raw freezing**. (Blanching is recommended if freezing whole, pg 48). Note that freezing onions results in a slightly softer texture once thawed, which is better for cooked dishes rather than raw. Onions also have a strong aroma even once frozen— they can smell up your freezer— so we favour putting ours in sealed containers rather than just freezer bags to combat their aroma.

TO USE: Can cook directly from frozen.
Use for adding flavour to your cooking (not for raw use). Sauté and add to soups, stews, chili, rice dishes, casseroles, or baked dishes.

CANNING It is not recommended to pressure can onions.

DEHYDRATING YOUR ONIONS

Onions take around 4-12 hours to dehydrate, depending on their thickness and moisture content. Peel skin and discard ends. Slice thinly or dice. Dehydrating steps, pg 63

TO USE: Add dehydrated onions directly to soups, stews, chili, rice dishes, casseroles, or baked dishes. Incorporate them directly into dips, sauces, or salad dressings or add them to your eggs. Grind dehydrated onions into onion powder and use them as a seasoning (pg 67) or as an ingredient in homemade spice blends or rubs. This adds an oniony flavour to your seasoning mix. Rehydrate them by soaking them in hot water for about 15-30 minutes before adding them to recipes that require sautéing or simmering.

FERMENTING YOUR ONIONS

Fermenting onions creates a probiotic-rich, tangy condiment that can be used in salads and sandwiches, or mixed into dips and sauces. Peel skin and discard ends. Slice or chop as desired. Fermenting steps, pg 74

TO USE: Add fermented onions to your favourite sandwiches, wraps, tacos, quesadillas, or hot dogs for a burst of flavour. They work well with both cold and hot items. Add to green salads, potato salads, or pasta salads for a tangy twist. Stir fermented onions into vegetables or stir-fries just before serving. Add to rice or grain dishes, pilafs, risottos, or quinoa for added flavour, or incorporate fermented onions into stuffed vegetables, such as bell peppers or mushrooms, for a tangy filling.

PICKLING YOUR ONIONS

Pickled onions are incredibly versatile, and there are numerous variations you can try to flavour your dishes (such as sweet pickled, cider + honey pickled, sesame ginger pickled) to enjoy throughout the year. Pickling red onions turns them a delightfully pink colour. Peel skin and discard ends. Slice or chop as desired. Pickling steps, pg 80 or 81
Processing time (water bath canning):10 min

TO USE: Pickled onions are a vibrant addition to salads, sandwiches, wraps, hot dogs, burgers or tacos. Add them to grilled cheese, grain bowls, Buddha bowls, or poke bowls. Or serve alongside fish, shrimp, or seafood dishes or grilled meats. Spread pickled onions over avocado toast to add acidity and flavour, or sprinkle over your eggs, omelets, or frittatas for a tangy kick. Float a few pickled onion slices on top of soups, especially those with a creamy or savoury base. Stir pickled onions into potato salad for an extra layer of flavour. Add to dips, sushi rolls, or include on charcuterie boards.

SHALLOTS
—

Edible bulbs with delicate, soft onion flavour.

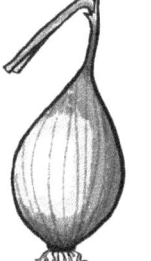

Shallots are enjoyed both raw and cooked. They add a nuanced, soft onion flavour to recipes, and they can be used in dressings, dips, sauces, and other cooking. Loosen the bulb to separate the cloves. Trim the bottoms and peel away the papery skin to access the flavourful, edible clove. Mince, chop, or slice to use.

FRESH STORAGE — Store shallots in a cool, dry, dark place such as the pantry, back of a cupboard, or the garage. Store in an open paper bag, basket, or bucket without a lid so the air can circulate around them in storage. Lasts up to a year.

QUICK TIP — Shallots pair exceptionally well with seafood, steak, and ingredients like garlic, white wine, tarragon, dijon, parsley, lemon, spinach, asparagus, green beans, and beets.

PRESERVATION — Freeze, dehydrate, ferment, or pickle.
Follow methods for preserving onions (pg 220)

FLOWERS

Vegetables // grown for their flowers

BROCCOLI
—

Large edible flower with grassy, vegetal flavour.

 Florets and stems are edible and versatile. Enjoy them raw in salads or with dip. You can steam, roast, pan-fry them, or add to stir fry, soups, casseroles, or pasta.

 Stem is delicious and nutritious and can be added to anything you use the florets for. If you find the outer skin tough, you can peel it with a vegetable peeler.

FRESH STORAGE	Store in the refrigerator in a plastic bag (or container) with the top cracked open for a bit of air circulation. Broccoli produces ethylene gas, which causes it to ripen quicker, so keeping it wrapped while still allowing some air to escape is best. Lasts a week or two.
QUICK TIP	Broccoli pairs well with chicken, salmon, duck, pork, and beef, along with ingredients like cauliflower, carrots, green beans, cheddar, rice, pasta, tofu, almonds, cashews, feta, and goat cheese.
PRESERVATION	Freeze, dehydrate, ferment, or pickle. (See next page for more)

FREEZING YOUR BROCCOLI

You can freeze your broccoli blanched or cooked. **Blanching is a crucial step** (pg 48) to preserve the colour, flavour, and texture of broccoli. Freeze cut into florets of desired size.

TO USE: Can cook directly from frozen.
Add frozen broccoli to stir fries, noodle dishes, casseroles, soups, stews, rice bowls, or pasta dishes. Steam or microwave frozen broccoli and serve it as a simple and healthy side dish season it with salt, pepper, and a squeeze of lemon juice, or make a quick cheese sauce and pour it over. Roast frozen broccoli on a sheet pan along with other vegetables and proteins for an easy, quick one-pan meal.

CANNING It is not recommended to pressure can broccoli.

DEHYDRATING YOUR BROCCOLI

Broccoli takes around 8-12 hours to dehydrate, depending on thickness and moisture content. Cut the broccoli into small, uniform florets to dehydrate. Blanch 3 minutes. Dehydrating steps, pg 63

TO USE: Add dehydrated broccoli directly to soups and stews, it will rehydrate during the cooking process. You can also rehydrate broccoli by soaking it in hot water for 15-30 minutes. Add rehydrated broccoli to stir fries, casseroles, pasta dishes, omelets, frittatas, rice, or grain bowls.

FERMENTING YOUR BROCCOLI

Fermenting broccoli creates a probiotic-rich, tangy item that can be added to various dishes. Cut into florets. Fermenting steps, pg 74

TO USE: Enjoy fermented broccoli as a flavorful side dish on its own. Add it to salads for an extra burst of flavour or into sandwiches, wraps, pitas, and grilled cheese for a zesty kick to your favourite lunchtime options. Include in grain bowls, combining it with rice, quinoa, or other grains along with your favourite proteins and sauces. Incorporate fermented broccoli into omelets or frittatas, adding a savoury and tangy note to your breakfast. Toss it into pasta dishes; it complements various pasta sauces, from simple garlic and olive oil to creamy alfredo.

PICKLING YOUR BROCCOLI

Broccoli can be pickled for a tasty and crunchy addition to salads, sandwiches, and more to be enjoyed throughout the year. Try various flavour combinations by experimenting with different spices like mustard seeds, dill, or red pepper flakes. Cut into florets. Pickling steps, pg 80 or 81
Processing time (water bath canning):10 min

TO USE: Toss pickled broccoli into green salads or grain salads for an extra burst of flavor. Include in sandwiches, wraps, pitas, grain bowls. Serve alongside grilled meats or add to cold noodle or pasta salad.

BRUSSELS SPROUTS

—

Edible buds with an earthy, slightly bitter flavour.

 Entire bud is edible and nutritious. Enjoy raw or cooked. Use shredded in salads or sautéed with onions and a squeeze of lemon, steamed whole, sliced in halves and roasted, or added to stews or casseroles.

 Trim the tip and discard, as well as any wilting outer leaves.

FRESH STORAGE	Loose brussels sprouts should be stored unwashed in a sealed bag or container in the refrigerator. Lasts a week.
	Keep brussels sprouts on the stalk if you received them this way. Trim the end of the stalk and prop it in a jar of water, store this way in the refrigerator (refreshing water as needed) until ready to use. Lasts up to a month.
QUICK TIP	Brussels sprouts pair well with bacon, beef, ham, and duck, along with ingredients like apples, garlic, ginger, onions, orange, dried cranberries, nuts, blue cheese, and parmesan.
PRESERVATION	Freeze, dehydrate, ferment, or pickle. (See next page for more)

FREEZING YOUR BRUSSELS SPROUTS

You can freeze your brussels sprouts raw, blanched, or cooked (pg 48).
Freeze them whole (ends trimmed), halved, or chopped, depending on your purpose.

TO USE: Can cook directly from frozen.
Toss frozen brussels sprouts with olive oil, salt, and pepper, and roast them in the oven until they are golden brown and crispy (add garlic or parmesan cheese) to serve as a side. Pan fry or sauté. Add them to stir-frys or casseroles, or use in sheet pan meals. Make a hash by sautéing frozen Brussels sprouts with potatoes, onions, and your choice of protein, and top with a fried or poached egg for a complete meal.

CANNING It is not recommended to pressure can brussels sprouts.

DEHYDRATING YOUR BRUSSELS SPROUTS

Brussels sprouts take around 6-12 hours to dehydrate, depending on their size and moisture content. Boil or steam them whole until crisp tender, then cool in a bowl of ice water. Cut into halves or slice thinly (smaller pieces will dehydrate more quickly).
Dehydrating steps, pg 63

TO USE: Rehydrate brussels sprouts before using them, by soaking them in warm water for about 30 minutes. Enjoy rehydrated brussels sprouts roasted, tossed in pasta dishes, casseroles, added to salads, stir frys, omelets, or frittatas, or as a pizza topping.

FERMENTING YOUR BRUSSELS SPROUTS

Fermented brussels sprouts have a tangy and slightly effervescent taste. They can be used in salads and sandwiches, mixed into dips and sauces, or as a side dish. Remove any loose or damaged outer leaves and trim the ends. Leave whole, cut in half, or shredded as desired. Fermenting steps, pg 74

TO USE: Chop fermented brussels sprouts and add them to salads for a burst of tangy flavor. They pair well with both leafy greens and grains. Include them in sandwiches, wraps, or pitas. Add fermented brussels sprouts to stir-fries for a unique and tangy twist. They can be tossed in towards the end of cooking to preserve their crunch. Use as a pizza topping. Mix fermented brussels sprouts into coleslaw for a unique and tangy twist on this classic side dish. Serve them as a side dish alongside roasted meats or other main courses, or incorporate them into quiches or savoury tarts.

PICKLING YOUR BRUSSELS SPROUTS

Brussels sprouts can be plain pickled or flavoured in any number of sweet or savoury pickle variations (such as garlic dill pickled, chipotle pickled, maple balsamic pickled) to enjoy throughout the year. Pickle whole or halved. Pickling steps, pg 80 or 81
Processing time (water bath canning): 10 min

TO USE: Chop pickled brussels sprouts and add them to salads for a tangy and crunchy element. They work well with mixed greens, nuts, and vinaigrettes. Add them to grain bowls, tacos, quesadillas, pasta salads, or coleslaws. Top burgers or sliders with pickled brussels sprouts to replace traditional pickles. Incorporate them into fried rice for a flavorful and tangy twist.

CABBAGE
—

Dense-leafed head with crunchy, slightly sweet flavour.

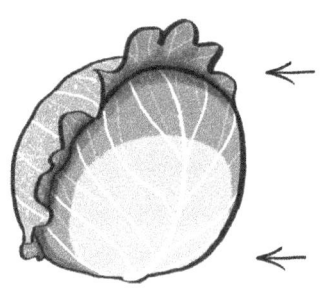

Leaves are enjoyed both raw and cooked. They have a tender crunch and slightly peppery flavour when eaten raw (shredded or sliced into coleslaws, salads, tacos) and a soft, sweetened flavour when cooked (soups, stews, roasted in wedges, sauteed). This nutritious vegetable holds up well, no matter how you use it.

Stem and inner core are woody and can be discarded.

FRESH STORAGE	Store unwashed and whole in a sealed plastic bag in the refrigerator until ready to use. It will store for months this way. Peel off and discard the outer leaves as they age.
QUIRKS	Cabbage comes in different varieties with looser or tighter packed heads. Summer cabbage heads are looser and more tender and typically eaten within weeks of harvest. Fall and winter cabbage heads have dense, tightly compact leaves and can be stored for many months.
PRESERVATION	Freeze, dehydrate, ferment, or pickle. (See next page for more)

FREEZING YOUR CABBAGE

You can freeze your cabbage blanched or cooked. **Blanching is a crucial step** to preserve the color, flavor, and texture of cabbage (pg 48). Freeze it shredded or in wedges depending on your purpose. Note that freezing cabbage results in a softer texture once thawed, still a delicious addition to cooked dishes, not recommended for raw use such as salads.

TO USE: Can cook directly from frozen.
Toss into soups, stews, stir fries, casseroles, fried rice, or curries. Sauté with other frozen vegetables to create a vegetable medley. Make cabbage rolls by stuffing blanched and thawed cabbage leaves with a mixture of meat, rice, and seasonings and baked in tomato sauce for a comforting meal.

CANNING YOUR CABBAGE

While you can preserve cabbage through **pressure canning,** it's important to note that the texture of cabbage softens significantly, and the flavour becomes quite strong. If you are interested in canning cabbage, **the recommended method is to pickle it.** Pressure canning steps, pg 57   **Processing time: 75 min (pints) 90 min (quarts)**

DEHYDRATING YOUR CABBAGE

Cabbage takes around 6-12 hours to dehydrate, depending on thickness. Cut into thin strips. Dehydrating steps, pg 63

TO USE: Add dehydrated cabbage directly to soups, stews, casseroles, or stir fries-- it will rehydrate during cooking. Or you can rehydrate it by soaking it in warm water for 15-30 minutes before adding it to your recipes. Incorporate rehydrated cabbage into Asian dishes, such as noodle bowls, spring rolls, or dumplings, or you can toss it into salads. The texture won't be as crisp as fresh cabbage but still contribute to the overall flavour profile.

FERMENTING YOUR CABBAGE

One of the most popular ways to ferment cabbage is by making sauerkraut (German sour cabbage). Another popular way is to make kimchi, a traditional Korean fermented vegetable dish. Kimchi typically includes napa cabbage, but you can substitute any cabbage in combination with other vegetables. Both ferments are simple to prepare and add a burst of flavour and a dose of healthy probiotics to dishes. Fermenting steps, pg 74

TO USE: Add your fermented cabbage (sauerkraut or kimchi) to fried rice as a flavorful topping for tacos or as a filling for wraps. Serve alongside grilled sausages and pierogies, add to grilled cheese, quesadillas, and pizza, or use in a classic Reuben sandwich.

PICKLING YOUR CABBAGE

Cabbage can be plain pickled or flavoured in any number of sweet or savoury pickle variations (such as turmeric pickled, pickled with apple, citrus pickled, spicy pickled). Pickling steps, pg 80 or 81

Processing time (water bath canning):20 min

TO USE: Add pickled cabbage to tacos, burritos, burgers, sandwiches, or hot dogs. It pairs well with grilled meats, fish, or beans. Mix pickled cabbage into green salads, grain salads, or coleslaw for added flavour and texture. Add pickled cabbage to rice bowls or grain bowls for a burst of flavour. Combine it with proteins like grilled chicken, tofu, or shrimp. Serve it alongside barbecue dishes. Add to noodles dishes or cold noodle salads. Use pickled cabbage as a garnish for soups, especially those with a clear broth, to add a refreshing crunch and tang.

CAULIFLOWER

—

Head of tightly bunched florets with mild, nutty flavour.

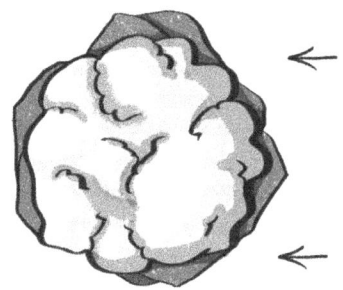

← Florets and their stems are edible and versatile. Chop and enjoy them raw in salads or with dip. Steam, roast, or pan-fry them, add them to stir-fry, soups, casseroles, or pasta, or roast the head whole drizzled with oil and seasonings.

← Stem and leaves are edible and nutritious too and can be added to anything you use the florets for. Stems can be peeled if you find the outer skin tough.

FRESH STORAGE	Store whole and unwashed in the refrigerator in a plastic bag (or container) with the top cracked open for a bit of air circulation. Lasts 2-3 weeks.
QUICK TIP	Cauliflower pairs well with beef, pork, and chickpeas, as well as ingredients like yogurt, turmeric, spices, curry, broccoli, carrots, asparagus, bok choy, cheddar, rice, and nuts.
PRESERVATION	Freeze, dehydrate, ferment, or pickle. (See next page for more)

FREEZING YOUR CAULIFLOWER

You can freeze your cauliflower raw, blanched, or cooked. **Blanching is recommended** to preserve the texture (pg 48). Cut the cauliflower into florets of your desired size to freeze.

TO USE: Can cook directly from frozen.
Boil or steam frozen cauliflower to serve as a side. Enjoy plain or smothered in creamy cheese sauce. Turn it into creamy cauliflower soup, cauliflower mash or cheesy cauliflower bake. Add to stir fries, casseroles, or curries. Roast or sauté frozen cauliflower with taco seasoning and use it as a filling for tacos or wraps. Mix frozen cauliflower into your favourite mac and cheese recipe for added nutrition and a veggie boost.

CANNING It is not recommended to pressure can cauliflower.

DEHYDRATING YOUR CAULIFLOWER

Cauliflower takes around 8-12 hours to dehydrate, depending on size. Cut the cauliflower into small, uniform florets to dehydrate. Dehydrating steps, pg 63

TO USE: You can rehydrate the cauliflower by soaking it in warm water for about 15-30 minutes before using it in recipes. Add to soups, stews, casseroles, gratins, stir fries, or curries. Mix rehydrated cauliflower with other vegetables for a veggie medley, either roasted, steamed or sautéed.

FERMENTING YOUR CAULIFLOWER

Fermenting cauliflower creates a probiotic-rich, tangy condiment that can be used in salads, sandwiches, or as a zesty, crunchy snack. Cut into florets. Fermenting steps, pg 74

TO USE: Enjoy it as a snack straight from the jar. Serve as a side dish alongside your favourite main courses. Add to salads, sandwiches, wraps, tacos, or burritos for a tangy, crunchy kick. Add to stir fries or buddha bowls. Top soups, especially creamy ones, with a spoonful of fermented cauliflower for added flavour and probiotics. Blend it with other ingredients like yogurt, garlic, and herbs to create a probiotic-rich dip or spread.

PICKLING YOUR CAULIFLOWER

Cauliflower can be plain pickled or flavoured in any number of sweet or savoury pickle variations (such as garlic + dill pickled, taco-spiced pickled, mediterranean pickled) to enjoy throughout the year. Cut into florets. Pickling steps, pg 80 or 81
Processing time (water bath canning):10 min

TO USE: Enjoy pickled cauliflower straight from the jar as a tasty and tangy snack. Include it on a charcuterie or appetizer board alongside cheeses, cured meats, and other pickled vegetables. Add to salads, sandwiches, wraps, tacos, burritos, or buddha bowls. Chop pickled cauliflower and mix it into egg salad or chicken salad for a zesty upgrade, or add to pasta salad for an extra layer of flavour. Create a hummus bowl topped with pickled cauliflower, cherry tomatoes, olives, and a drizzle of olive oil.

ROMANESCO
—

Head of spire-like florets with nutty flavour.

← Florets and stems are edible and versatile. Chop and enjoy them raw in salads or with dip. Steam, roast, or pan-fry them, add them to stir-fry, soups, casseroles, or pasta, or roast the head whole drizzled with oil and seasonings.

← Stem and leaves are edible too and can be added to anything you use the florets for. Stems can be peeled with a vegetable peeler if you find the outer skin tough.

FRESH STORAGE	Store whole and unwashed in the refrigerator in a plastic bag (or container) with the top cracked open for a bit of air circulation. Lasts 2-3 weeks.
QUICK TIP	Romanesco pairs well with ingredients like garlic, lemon, yogurt, capers, spices, pasta, parmesan, nuts and sharp cheeses (like feta, blue cheese, goat cheese, and gouda).
PRESERVATION	Freeze, dehydrate, ferment, or pickle. Follow methods for cauliflower (pg 240).

FRUITS

Vegetables // grown for their fruit

CUCUMBER

—

Crisp cylindrical vegetable with cool, refreshing flavour.

 The top portion of the cucumber, nearest the stem, contains the most bitter portion. Slice and discard the first inch or two. (Learn more about cucumber bitterness below)

 Cucumbers are generally eaten raw, sliced in sandwiches, salads, or as a raw snack. Their high water content gives them a mild, slightly sweet flavour. They vary in size, length, and skin texture. Those with thicker skins can be peeled. Cucumbers are also commonly pickled (pg 80).

FRESH STORAGE   Store in a sealed plastic bag in the warmest part of your refrigerator. Once sliced, wrap the cucumber in plastic wrap to prevent it from losing moisture. Lasts up to 2 weeks, though its life span shortens once cut.

QUIRKS   Cucumbers sometimes taste bitter because of cucurbitacin, a chemical in the plant that wards off predators but sometimes works its way down the stem into the vegetable. While it is okay to eat, it tastes unpleasant. This bitter compound is concentrated mainly towards the stem end of the cucumber.

HOW TO: To reduce cucumber bitterness, slice off the first inch or two of the stem end, then vigorously rub the cut ends against each other to draw out the white foamy bitterness. Rinse and use. You can also pickle your bitter cucumbers (pg 80), which balances any bitterness.

PRESERVATION   Dehydrate, ferment, or pickle.
(See next page for more)

FREEZING It is not recommended to freeze cucumbers, as once thawed, they become watery mush. Frozen cucumbers are only usable for cold puréed soups (gazpacho), smoothies, or beverages.

CANNING It is not recommended to pressure can cucumbers.

DEHYDRATING YOUR CUCUMBERS

Cucumbers take around 6-10 hours to dehydrate, depending on the thickness. Slice thinly into rounds or chopped pieces. Dehydrating steps, pg 63

TO USE: Enjoy dehydrated cucumber chips as a crunchy snack, they make a great alternative to traditional chips. Combine with nuts, seeds, and dried fruits for a crunchy trail mix. Make infused water by adding a few dehydrated cucumber slices for subtle cucumber flavor. Crush dehydrated cucumber slices into a powder and mix it into yogurt, cream cheese, or hummus to create a cucumber-infused spread or dip. Sprinkle dehydrated cucumber slices on top of cold soups like gazpacho for a delightful crunch. Rehydrate the cucumber slices by soaking them in water for a few minutes, and add them to salads, wraps, or sandwiches. Or try combining rehydrated cucumber slices with tomatoes, onions, cilantro, lime juice, and spices to create a unique cucumber salsa to serve with tortilla chips or as a topping for grilled meats or fish.

FERMENTING YOUR CUCUMBERS

Cucumbers are commonly fermented as pickles. The process of fermenting cucumbers involves placing them in a brine solution of salt, water, and various spices, allowing beneficial bacteria to naturally ferment the cucumbers, which produce the characteristic tangy pickle flavour with all the probiotic benefits. Fermenting steps, pg 74

TO USE: Enjoy as a snack straight from the jar or in all the ways you would regular pickled cucumbers (see below).

PICKLING YOUR CUCUMBERS

One of the most common preserves, cucumbers can be pickled and flavoured in any number of variations (such as dill pickled, bread + butter pickled, spicy pickled) to enjoy throughout the year. Pickling steps, pg 80 or 81 **Processing time (water bath canning):15 min**

TO USE: Enjoy your pickles straight from the jar as a tasty snack. Add to sandwiches, burgers, wraps, or grilled cheese. Serve them as part of a charcuterie board; they pair well with various meats, cheeses, and condiments. Mix chopped pickles with mayonnaise, mustard, and herbs to create a flavorful tartar sauce to serve with fish and seafood, or finely chop them up on their own for a simple tangy relish to use on hot dogs, sausages, or grilled meats. Add chopped pickles to potato salads, egg salads, or green salads for a zesty twist (the pickle brine can also be used as part of the dressing). Blend pickles with cream cheese, sour cream, or yogurt to create a tangy dip or spread (use for vegetables, crackers, or pretzels).

Use pickle brine in cocktails, such as a pickle martini or a pickle-infused Bloody Mary, to add a savoury and tangy kick to your drink. Use the brine as a base for sauces or marinades to add depth and tanginess to barbecue sauces, salad dressings, or marinades for grilled meats. Pickle brine can also be used as part of salad dressing (pg 85).

EGGPLANT
—

Glossy purple vegetable with meaty white flesh.
(aka. Aubergine)

 Peel or slice off the green top and discard.

 Edible with skin on, though the skin becomes bitter with age, so you may want to peel older eggplants. This mild, flavoured vegetable comes in many sizes and colours. It can be broiled, grilled, pan-fried, stuffed, or baked, and is especially delicious breaded, fried and smothered in cheese and marinara sauce (Eggplant Parmigiana). You can also roast and purée the flesh (see below) for use in dips (Baba Ghanoush), soups, stews, and sauces.

FRESH STORAGE Do not store in plastic, it likes to breathe. Eggplants do not like it too warm or too cold, so ideal storage is in a dark pantry or on your countertop out of sunlight. Do not store near high-ethalyne produce (bananas, apples, or onions) as it will accelerate deterioration. Lasts 2 weeks.

QUICK TIP Eggplant pairs well with beef and lamb, as well as ingredients like sesame, tahini, olives, garlic, capers, fresh herbs, zucchini, red wine, tomatoes, mozzarella, goat cheese, parmesan, and nuts.

EASY EGGPLANT PUREE: Roast eggplant whole by piercing all over with a fork and placing on a baking sheet in 400° oven. Roast for 40 minutes or until flesh is soft when pierced with a fork. Slice in half and scoop out the flesh. Pulse flesh in a food processor until smooth. Refrigerate or freeze until use. Discard skins.

PRESERVATION Freeze, dehydrate, or pickle.
(See next page for more)

FREEZING YOUR EGGPLANT

You can freeze your eggplant blanched or cooked (pg 48).
Freezing will create a softer texture once thawed, so plan to use it in cooked dishes where the texture is not the focus (such as sauces, stews, or casseroles). **I recommend freezing your eggplant cooked,** such as oven-baked slices, roasted pieces, or purée (pg 250).

TO USE: Cook directly from frozen.
Use frozen eggplant in casseroles or baked dishes like moussaka or eggplant parmesan. The freezing process softens the eggplant, making it suitable for layering in these comforting dishes. Add directly to stir-fries (the slightly softer texture won't be as noticeable in the mix of other ingredients, and it will absorb flavours well). Toss frozen eggplant into soups, stews (such as classic ratatouille, or curries, or blend it into pasta sauces to add a rich and creamy texture. Use it as a pizza topping, or roast/grill it with other vegetables.

CANNING It is not recommended to pressure can eggplant.

DEHYDRATING YOUR EGGPLANT

Eggplant takes around 4-12 hours to dehydrate, depending on thickness of slices and moisture content. You can leave the skin on or peel it off. To make eggplant chips (also known as "eggplant bacon" or "vegan jerky"), slice thinly and season with your favourite spices before dehydrating for a healthy and flavourful snack. Dehydrating steps, pg 63

TO USE: Soak the dehydrated eggplant slices in hot water (or broth) for 20-30 minutes to rehydrate them before adding them to recipes. Use in soups, stews, or casseroles such as eggplant parmesan or moussaka, pasta primavera, ratatouille, or eggplant lasagna. Toss into vegetarian stir-fries, it will absorb the flavors and add unique texture to the dish. Add to vegetarian chili, curry, use as a pizza topping, or blend with other ingredients to make dip or spread.

PICKLING YOUR EGGPLANT

Eggplant can be plain pickled or flavoured in any number of sweet or savoury pickle variations (such as garlic + herb pickled, italian pickled, sesame + soy sauce pickled) to enjoy throughout the year. Slice into rounds or sticks. Pickling steps, pg 80 or 81
Processing time (water bath canning):10 min

TO USE: Add pickled eggplant to sandwiches or wraps for a tangy, flavorful kick. It pairs well with deli meats, cheeses, and fresh greens. Make an antipasto platter by arranging pickled eggplant slices with other pickled vegetables, olives, cheeses, and cured meats. Toss into green salads, pasta salads, or grain salads for a burst of flavour. Spread pickled eggplant on toasted bread for a quick and tasty bruschetta or crostini (top with fresh herbs for added freshness). Mix into pasta dishes with tomato-based sauces or olive oil-based sauces like spaghetti or penne. Add to grain bowls for a zesty element (use grains like quinoa, farro, or couscous). Include pickled eggplant on a mezze platter alongside hummus, tzatziki, falafel, and pita bread for a Mediterranean-inspired appetizer. Blend pickled eggplant with garlic, olive oil, and tahini to create a flavorful eggplant dip (serve with pita chips or fresh vegetables).

FERMENTING It is not recommended to ferment eggplant. Due to its high water content, it will turn mushy during the process.

GEM SQUASH

—

Small, round vegetable with sweet-tasting flesh.

← Remove and discard stem.

← Somewhere between a summer squash and a winter squash, gem squash skin is soft and edible when picked young and coarse and inedible when picked later in season. Gem squashes are commonly baked whole or roasted in halves with seeds scooped out and stuffed with a delicious filling.

FRESH STORAGE — Do not store in plastic, it likes to breathe. Store in a cool, dry, dark place (back of a cupboard, in a closet, or garage). When picked young (soft skin), they last 2 weeks. If matured to a hard skin before being picked, they will last months.

QUICK TIP — Gem squash pairs well with ingredients like corn, garlic, fresh herbs, spices, cheese (cheddar, parmesan, brie, gorgonzola, mozzarella), honey, and nuts.

PRESERVATION — Freeze, pressure can, dehydrate, ferment, or pickle.
(See next page for more)

FREEZING YOUR GEM SQUASH

You can freeze your gem squash raw, blanched, or cooked (pg 48).
Freeze whole, halved, quartered (seeds scooped out, peeled if desired), or in desired-size portions depending on your purpose. The texture will be slightly different from fresh squash, but freezing is an excellent way to preserve for later use.

TO USE: Thaw in the refrigerator before cooking.
Mash or purée with salt, pepper, and a bit of butter for a simple side dish. Add to soups, stews, curries, or casseroles for a creamy and nutritious element. Use in savoury pies or quiches. Make into fritters or patties: mix thawed gem squash with grated cheese, breadcrumbs, and herbs and pan-fry until golden brown. Blend into pasta sauce, adding a subtle sweetness. Incorporate into baked dishes like lasagna, enchiladas, or stuffed peppers. Add to smoothies for a nutrient boost (it pairs well with fruits like bananas and berries).

CANNING YOUR GEM SQUASH

You can preserve gem squash through **pressure canning** for use in your favourite recipes or as a side dish. Peel and cut them into small, manageable pieces (seeds scooped out) before placing them in jars. Pressure canning steps, pg 57
Processing time: 55 min (pints) 90 min (quarts)

DEHYDRATING YOUR GEM SQUASH

Gem squash takes around 7-12 hours to dehydrate, depending on thickness of the slices. You can peel the gem squash if you prefer, or dehydrate it with the skin on. Dehydrating steps, pg 63

TO USE: Add dehydrated gem squash to soups, stews, or chili. It will absorb the flavors of the broth and add a hearty texture to the dish. Soak dehydrated pieces in warm water for 20 minutes to rehydrate. Add rehydrated gem squash to risotto, use as a pizza topping, or mix with herbs and spices to create a flavorful filling for turnovers or hand pies.

FERMENTING YOUR GEM SQUASH

Fermenting gem squash is less common than other vegetables, but it is technically possible. Experiment with small batches to achieve the flavour and texture you prefer. Fermenting steps, pg 74

PICKLING YOUR GEM SQUASH

Gem squash can be plain pickled or flavoured in any number of sweet or savoury pickle variations (such as honey + ginger pickled, curry pickled, spicy pickled) and is a delicious way to enjoy this vegetable throughout the year. Cut the gem squash (seeds scooped out, peeled if desired) into slices, wedges, or cubes. Pickling steps, pg 80 or 81
Processing time (water bath canning):10 min

TO USE: Pickled gem squash can be enjoyed as a side dish, a topping for salads, or a tangy snack. Include it in sandwiches, wraps, tacos or burritos for a burst of flavour. Add to charcuterie boards to compliment cheeses, cured meats, and crackers. Add to grain bowls or buddha bowls. Serve as a side dish for grilled meats or barbecue. Or chop pickled gem squash into smaller pieces and use it as a relish or salsa. It pairs well with grilled meats and fish or as a topping for tacos.

PEPPERS
—

Crunchy, juicy vegetable with energetic, snappy flavour.

 Cut out stems, white spongy centers, and seeds. Discard.

 Enjoy both raw and cooked. Serve chopped or sliced in salads, wraps, fresh salsas, or as a snack. Use as a simple addition to any cooked dish, such as pasta, soups, stews, filling for fajitas, or as a pizza topping. You can also cut in halves and stuff with fillings and bake. For enhanced flavour, try roasting and peeling them before use (pg260).

FRESH STORAGE   Ensure they are dry (moisture leads to early spoilage), and store them whole in the refrigerator (in the crisper drawer) inside a plastic bag with holes (or with the top left open) to allow for airflow. Once cut, store in a sealed bag or container with a folded paper towel to absorb excess moisture). Lasts 2 weeks.

QUIRKS   Peppers come in all heat levels, from sweetly mild to flaming hot! Know which type of pepper you have before biting into it, or you may regret it. The widely used scale for measuring heat in peppers is called The Scoville Scale, which has categories of mild, medium, hot, extra hot, and extremely hot. Look it up to learn the level of your pepper.

Wear disposable gloves when cutting hot peppers, and avoid touching your eyes, nose or mouth to prevent burning pain.

RELIEF: If you get pepper juice in your eyes or on skin, apply milk to the burning area to soothe the pain (do not use water; it simply spreads the heat). The heat and pain will eventually fade.

PRESERVATION   Freeze, pressure can, dehydrate, ferment, or pickle.
(See next page for more)

How to Peel Peppers

Peppers can be blistered and skins peeled off before preserving.
This is optional, but pepper skin becomes tough and unpleasant, especially when canned. HOW TO: Slice peppers in half, then core and seed. Place cut-side down on foil-lined or parchment-lined baking sheet. Broil for 6-8 minutes until skins are wrinkled and charred. Transfer to a bowl and cover tightly with a lid, plastic wrap, or a plate. Allow to sweat for 30 minutes. Peel away skins and discard.

FREEZING YOUR PEPPERS

You can freeze your peppers raw or cooked (pg 48), no need to blanch.
Freeze peppers in slices, strips, or dice, or as stuffed peppers, depending on your purpose. Alternatively, you can roast and peel first (see above) for additional flavour. Freezing results in a softer texture once thawed which is best for use in cooked dishes.

TO USE: Can cook directly from frozen.
Toss frozen pepper strips or slices directly into stir-fries. Add to soups, stews, casseroles or baked dishes. Throw frozen pepper strips into omelets or scrambled eggs, add to pasta sauces, or use as a pizza topping. Cook frozen pepper slices with onions for quick and easy fajitas or taco fillings. You can use them in grilled or roasted dishes, just be aware that they may release more moisture during cooking.

FERMENTING YOUR PEPPERS

Fermenting peppers is a popular method for preserving and creating probiotic-rich, tangy products like hot sauces and pickled peppers. (Note: Extremely hot peppers won't ferment because the high level of capsaicin in them.) Fermenting steps, pg 74

TO USE: Blend the fermented peppers with some of the brine to create a homemade hot sauce (depending on the spiciness of the pepper variety). Adjust the thickness by adding more brine if needed. Add fermented peppers to barbecue sauces, aiolis, vinaigrettes, hummus, or dips for a flavorful and tangy twist. Finely chop or blend fermented peppers to make salsas, guacamole, or spicy dips. Include in marinades for meats, tofu, or vegetables. Add to sandwiches, wraps, pizza, grain bowls, casseroles, green salads, pasta salads, or potato salads.

DEHYDRATING YOUR PEPPERS

Peppers take around 6-12 hours to dehydrate, depending on their thickness and moisture content. For tough-skinned peppers, you may wish to remove the skin first (pg 260). unless you will be grinding them into powder afterwards. Slice into halves, rounds, thin strips, or small dice. Smaller pieces will dry faster. Dehydrating steps, pg 63

TO USE: Dehydrated peppers add a concentrated burst of flavour to your recipes. Grind dehydrated peppers into powder to create your own paprika or spice blends. Mix them with other dried herbs and spices to make a custom seasoning for meats, vegetables, or dips. Add them to rice or grain dishes while cooking for an extra burst of flavour (they work well in pilafs, risottos, and grain bowls). Crush or grind dehydrated peppers and add them to pasta sauces (particularly tomato-based sauces) for a spicy kick. Incorporate them into casseroles or baked dishes. Crush or finely chop dehydrated peppers and sprinkle them over pizza before baking for a spicy element. Rehydrate them by soaking them in hot water for about 15-30 minutes and add to homemade salsas, guacamole, or other dips.

CANNING YOUR PEPPERS

You can preserve peppers through **pressure canning** for delicious use in cooking. Peppers should be blistered and skins peeled off first (pg 260). Pressure canning steps, pg 57
Processing time: 35 min (pints or quarts)

PICKLING YOUR PEPPERS

Peppers can be plain pickled or flavoured in any number of sweet or savoury pickle variations (such as italian pickled, mustard pickled, habenero mango pickled) to enjoy throughout the year. You can pickle them whole, halved, or sliced. Tough-skinned varieties should be peeled first (pg 260). Pickling steps, pg 80 or 81
Processing time (water bath canning):10 min

TO USE: Layer pickled peppers in sandwiches, wraps, burgers, or hot dogs. Chop and toss them into green salads for added flavour and a hint of acidity. Scatter pickled peppers over nachos, tacos, and fajitas, or fold them into quesadillas for a spicy, tangy kick. Mix them into scrambled eggs, omelets, or frittatas. Serve as part of a cheese or charcuterie board. Stir chopped pickled peppers into tomato-based or creamy pasta sauces for a zesty kick, or add to potato salad, stir-fries, or grain bowls.

PUMPKIN

—

Globe-shaped vegetable with subtly sweet, earthy flavour.

← Knock off the stem and discard before baking. Pumpkin seeds can be scooped out, discarded, rinsed free of strings, and toasted with spices for a tasty snack.

← Pumpkin flesh is perfect for roasting, steaming, baking, or puréeing (pg 267) for use in sauces, muffins, pies etc. The flavour works well in both sweet and savoury dishes. To use your pumpkin, cut in half, scrape out seeds and strings with a metal spoon, and cook according to your recipe. Skin is edible, though generally not eaten.

FRESH STORAGE — Store in a cool, dry, dark place such as a pantry, back of a cupboard, or garage. Place on a shelf or open bin where the air can circulate around them. Store them away from apples, bananas, and onions (these ethylene-producing items will accelerate rotting). Lasts 2-3 months.

QUIRKS — Certain varieties are more delicious than others. Sugar pumpkins (smaller, round, orange pumpkins; pictured) are cultivated for their thicker, sweeter flesh and are ideal for cooking, baking, and pie-making.

Many varieties are not suitable for eating, known as ornamental pumpkins. Use these for decorative purposes only.

PRESERVATION — Freeze, pressure can, dehydrate, ferment, or pickle.
(See next page for more)

FREEZING YOUR PUMPKIN

You can freeze pumpkin raw, blanched, or cooked (pg 48).
Freeze pumpkin in cubes, chunks, or purée, depending on your purpose. Peel and seed it first. **Freeze purée in pre-portioned amounts** (such as 1 cup or 2 cups) based on what you plan to use it for. (See pumpkin purée instructions, pg 267)

TO USE: Can cook directly from frozen.
Add pumpkin chunks to soups, stews, or curries for a delicious autumn flavour. Pumpkin pairs well with flavours like ginger, nutmeg, and cinnamon. You can blend or process thawed pumpkin chunks into a smooth puree or use your pre-made purée in baking (cakes, muffins, breads, desserts), or for use in waffles, pancakes, risotto, ravioli filling, or pumpkin pasta sauce.

CANNING YOUR PUMPKIN

You can preserve blanched pumpkin chunks through **pressure canning**. (Do *not* can pumpkin purée; it is hazardous.) Peel the skin, scrape away seeds, and cut the pumpkin into cubes. Boil for 2 minutes before packing into jars. Pressure canning steps, pg 57
Processing time: 55 min (pints) 90 min (quarts)

FERMENTING YOUR PUMPKIN

Fermenting raw pumpkin creates a delicious and probiotic-rich item that can be used in many dishes. Peel, seed it, and cut into desired-size pieces. The fermentation process will naturally soften the pumpkin. Once it reaches the desired level of firmness, you can move the fermented pumpkin to the refrigerator to slow down the fermentation process. Fermenting steps, pg 74

TO USE: Spread fermented pumpkin on toasted baguette slices with fresh herbs or goat cheese for a tangy crostini. Toss pumpkin in salads, sandwiches, wraps, grain bowls, stir-fries, or tacos. Mash with yogurt, cream cheese, or hummus for a unique dip or spread.

DEHYDRATING YOUR PUMPKIN

Pumpkin takes around 8-12 hours to dehydrate, depending on the thickness of the pieces. To prevent discoloration, soak the pumpkin pieces in a solution of 1 tablespoon of lemon juice per 4 cups water for five minutes first. Dehydrating steps, pg 63

TO USE: Enjoy dehydrated pumpkin slices as a crunchy and healthy snack, or add them to homemade trail mix for a unique twist; season them with cinnamon, nutmeg, or pumpkin spice for extra flavour. Grind into powder and use as a natural flavouring in baked goods like muffins, pancakes, bread, or pumpkin spice latte. Make pumpkin spice butter by mixing pumpkin powder with softened butter, a bit of honey or maple syrup, and your favourite pumpkin spices to use as a spread for toast or pancakes. Add dehydrated pumpkin pieces or powder to homemade granola for a fall-inspired flavour. Soak dehydrated pumpkin in warm water to rehydrate and use in soups, stews, curries, or casseroles.

PICKLING YOUR PUMPKIN

Pumpkin can be plain pickled or flavoured in any number of sweet or savoury pickle variations (such as sweet + spicy pickled, mustard seed pickled, apple cider pickled) to enjoy throughout the year. Peel, seed it, and cut it into desired-size pieces. Pickling steps, pg 80 or 81 **Processing time (water bath canning): 20 min**

TO USE: Toss pickled pumpkin cubes or slices into salads with mixed greens, nuts, and cheese for a burst of flavour. Add to grain bowls (quinoa, rice, or couscous) along with other veggies and proteins. Use it as a topping for tacos or burritos. Serve pickled pumpkin alongside a cheese platter, or spread it on toasted baguette slices topped with goat cheese or ricotta for a flavorful crostini or bruschetta. Mix finely chopped pickled pumpkin into hummus or other creamy dips, or create a pumpkin relish with diced onions, tomatoes, and fresh herbs to serve alongside grilled meats or fish.

PERFECT PUMPKIN PURÉE

Have you ever baked with real pumpkin purée instead of the kind that comes in a can? The difference is unreal. You will not believe the fresh taste of your pies, muffins, and meals— it's a game changer. During autumn, I usually keep a stock on hand (stored in the refrigerator) to use whenever inspiration strikes. It gives a delicious fall flavour (and colour) to both meals and baking. Making it from scratch is easier than you might think.

Sugar pumpkin (or winter squash such as red curry, buttercup, blue hubbard, or kabocha)

Preheat oven to 375°
Knock off the stem of the squash or pumpkin (use a mallet or the edge of the counter) and discard. Stab with a fork in several places to allow steam to escape. Place in the oven whole. Bake for approximately 1 hour (depending on size) until the flesh is soft when pierced with a fork.

Remove from the oven (allow to cool before continuing if desired).

Slice in half. Gently scoop out seeds and strings and discard (or save and wash/dry seeds for toasting). Scoop out the flesh into a bowl (or directly into a food processor or blender). Puree until smooth, add water if needed for proper consistency.

Transfer to a sealed container and store in the refrigerator or freezer until ready to use. Purée can be stored in the refrigerator for up to a week or in the freezer for up to one year.

Use purée in soups, stews, casseroles, pasta sauces, muffins, cakes, pies, and more.

ROUND ZUCCHINI

Round, soft-skinned vegetable with dense, mellow flesh.

Stems are edible when cooked, though often removed and discarded. The younger and fresher the zucchini, the more tender the stem is. You can leave stems attached when cooking or slice them off to sauté or roast on their own.

Tastes and uses just like regular zucchini, but in a more fun shape! With soft edible skin, these short, fat summer squash are ideal for stuffing: Simply cut the zucchini in half and scoop out the center section to create little zucchini bowls; fill with your favourite filling and bake until tender. You can also use it in all the same ways you would use a regular zucchini (pg 284).

FRESH STORAGE	Store unwashed on the counter if using within a few days, or in the refrigerator for longer (in a crisper drawer or in a paper bag) to allow for air circulation. Lasts 2 weeks.
QUICK TIP	Round zucchini pairs well with meats and seafood, as well as ingredients like peppers, corn, basil, lemon, eggplant, garlic, onions, other summer squash, tomatoes, fresh herbs, nuts, cheeses (cheddar, parmesan, feta, ricotta), sour cream, and rice.
PRESERVATION	Freeze, dehydrate, ferment, or pickle. Follow methods for zucchini (pg 286).

SUMMER SQUASH

Soft-skinned, summer vegetable with dense, mellow flesh.

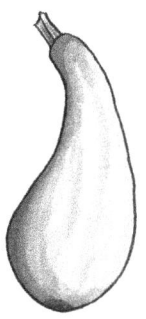

 Stems are edible when cooked, though frequently removed and discarded. The younger and fresher the squash, the more tender the stem is. You can leave stems attached when cooking or slice them off and sauté or roast on their own.

 Coming in various shapes and sizes, these lovely fellas can be roasted, pan-fried, grilled, or added to your soups, stir fries, pasta, or even shredded into baking. With soft, edible skin, they can be left whole, sliced into rounds, chopped up, or halved before cooking. They can be used in all the same ways you would use a zucchini (pg 284).

FRESH STORAGE — Store unwashed on the counter if using within a few days, or in the refrigerator for longer (in a crisper drawer or in a paper bag) to allow for air circulation. Lasts 2 weeks.

QUICK TIP — Round zucchini pairs well with meats and seafood, as well as ingredients like peppers, corn, basil, lemon, eggplant, garlic, onions, other summer squash, tomatoes, fresh herbs, nuts, cheeses (cheddar, parmesan, feta, ricotta), sour cream, and rice.

PRESERVATION — Freeze, dehydrate, ferment, or pickle.
Follow methods for zucchini (pg 286).

TOMATOES

Large juicy berries with sweet, tangy flavour.

← Stem is removed and discarded. Cut out the small core.

← With edible skin, these are enjoyed both raw and cooked. Add them raw to salads, sandwiches, wraps, or fresh salsas. Roast them in the oven, make them into sauce, or add them to soups, omelettes, or frittatas. Large amounts of tomatoes are commonly canned or preserved for use throughout the year. (Step by step canning, pg 56)

FRESH STORAGE If tomatoes are not yet ripe, store them on the counter for a few days until ripe. (Ripe tomatoes are fragrant and tender to the touch.) Once ripe, use it or store it in the refrigerator to preserve its freshness. Be sure it is ripened before putting it in the refrigerator or it will taste mealy and bland. Lasts 2 weeks.

QUIRKS Tomatoes are the only vegetable with high enough acidity to safely can without any specialized equipment (pg 56). Common ways of canning tomatoes include: diced tomatoes, crushed tomatoes, stewed tomatoes, and salsa.
(See pg 274 for tomato canning tips).

PRESERVATION Freeze, water bath or pressure can, dehydrate, ferment, or pickle.
(See next page for more)

How to Peel Tomatoes

The simplest way to prep your tomatoes for preservation.

While you can certainly just leave tomato skin on (it is edible and nutritious), peeling tomatoes is a common practice before canning. The skin has a tough, chewy texture that does not break down completely during cooking. Peeling tomatoes first will give you a smoother, more appealing texture in sauces, soups, salsas, and other dishes.

TO PEEL:
Cut out stem and core of each tomato with a melon baller or small knife. Freeze them whole (we pack them in sturdy bags and transfer them to the freezer). Allow at least 24 hours until frozen solid. When desired, take them straight from the freezer and dump directly into a clean sink. Turn the hot water on them. The peelings will slip off easily in your hands. You can chop the peeled tomatoes while still frozen or partially frozen.

>> Step by step canning, pg 56

Best tomato varieties for canning:
Roma, San Marzano, Amish Paste

You can certainly use any tomatoes you have for canning. However, oblong-shaped plum varieties hold up best and deliver a more concentrated flavour. With meaty flesh and low moisture content, these varieties produce a richer, thicker product.

FREEZING YOUR TOMATOES

You can freeze your tomatoes raw, blanched, or cooked.
Freeze them whole, puréed, chopped, or as soup or sauce, depending on your purpose. Frozen tomatoes do not have the same texture as fresh ones, but they are excellent for cooking and sauces. Peel tomatoes before use to improve texture and flavour. **I recommend freezing them whole** (with core + stem removed), then peeling and chopping them afterwards (pg 274)– it's super simple.

TO USE: Can cook directly from frozen.
Add frozen tomatoes to chili, stews, casseroles, curries, and slow-cooked dishes. Thaw tomatoes and simmer them with herbs, garlic, onions, and other seasonings to create a flavorful sauce or base for a soup. Remember to drain excess liquid if your frozen tomatoes release a lot of juice during thawing, especially if you want to control the consistency of your dish.

CANNING YOUR TOMATOES

You can preserve tomatoes through **pressure** or **water bath canning** as they are a high-acid food. It is recommended to peel them first (pg 274) to improve texture and flavour. Canning steps, pg 56 or 57   **Processing time: water bath canning 45 min (pints or quarts); pressure canning 25 min (pints or quarts)**

WAYS TO CAN TOMATOES: Whole, crushed, stewed, tomato soup, salsa, tomato juice, marinara sauce, pizza sauce, tomato relish, tomato jam, ketchup.

DEHYDRATING YOUR TOMATOES

Tomatoes take around 8-14 hours to dehydrate. Slice in halves, quarters, or smaller pieces. (Remove seeds and gel from the center.) Place them skin side down on tray.
Dehydrating steps, pg 63

TO USE: Enjoy as a snack, pizza topping, or finely chopped and incorporated into bread or focaccia dough. Soak in warm water or broth to rehydrate. Use in sauces, soups, stews, pasta dishes, or make tomato pesto.

FERMENTING YOUR TOMATOES

Fermenting tomatoes is less common than fermenting other vegetables, but it is possible to do so. Experiment with different herbs and spices to customize the flavour to your liking. Fermenting steps, pg 74

TO USE: Blend fermented tomatoes with garlic, basil, and olive oil to create a tangy, probiotic-rich tomato sauce. Chop or blend fermented tomatoes to make salsas or dips. Use them as a flavorful topping for tacos, nachos, or other Mexican-inspired dishes. Add to green salads, pasta salads, sandwiches, wraps, or burgers. Blend fermented tomatoes with olive oil, vinegar, and your favourite herbs to create a tangy vinaigrette for salads. Add to grain bowls or make a fermented tomato bruschetta.

PICKLING YOUR TOMATOES

Tomatoes can be plain pickled or flavoured in any number of sweet or savoury pickle variations (such as maple balsamic pickled, honey + ginger pickled, peppercorn pickled) to enjoy throughout the year. Pickling green tomatoes is a great way to use those unripe ones, creating a tangy and crisp condiment or side. Pickling steps, pg 80 or 81
Processing time (water bath canning):15 min

TO USE: Add pickled tomatoes to salads, sandwiches, wraps, or burgers, tacos, nachos, or quesadillas. Use as a topping for avocado toast, grilled meats, fish, or pasta dishes. Pair them with cheeses, or make into bruschetta.

WINTER SQUASH

Hard-skinned, fall vegetable with creamy, subtle flesh.

← Knock off stem and discard before baking.

← Winter squash are perfect for roasting, steaming, baking, or puréeing (pg 267) for use in sauces, muffins, pies etc. Their flavour works well in both sweet and savoury dishes. Some varieties have edible skin; others are best peeled or scooped from the skin (see below). To use, simply slice open, scrape away seeds and strings with a metal spoon and discard, then cook in your preferred way. Though they all taste similar, there are slight variations in texture and taste between them, with different varieties being more nutty, creamy, moist or dry.

FRESH STORAGE   Store in a cool, dry, dark place such as a pantry, back of a cupboard, basement, or garage. Place on a shelf or open bin where the air can circulate around them. Store them away from apples, bananas, and onions (these ethylene-producing items will accelerate rotting). Lasts 2-3 months.

QUIRKS   Some winter squash varieties have soft, edible skin, while others are best peeled or scooped from the skin after cooking.
(See next page for more on winter squash skins)

PRESERVATION   Freeze, pressure can, dehydrate, or pickle.
(See next page for more)

Soft Skin

WINTER SQUASH

Soft skin is edible and lovely to leave on when roasting. It adds visual appeal (especially sliced into rings or wedges with the seeds scooped out) and maintains a pleasing texture. Examples include:

Delicata
Acorn
Festival
Carnival
Honeynut
Sweet Dumpling

Hard Skin

WINTER SQUASH

Hard skin is coarse and best peeled away or with the tasty flesh scooped from the skin after cooking. These are typically roasted halved (seeds scooped out) or in wedges. Examples include:

Butternut
Kabocha
Spaghetti Squash
Red Kuri
Buttercup
Hubbard
Turban
Banana

FREEZING YOUR WINTER SQUASH

You can freeze winter squash raw, blanched, or cooked (pg 48).
Freeze in slices, wedges, cubes, or purée, depending on your purpose. Soft-skinned varieties don't need to be peeled first (pg 281). **Freeze purées in pre-portioned amounts** (such as 1 cup or 2 cups) based on what you plan to use it for (pg 267).

TO USE: Can cook directly from frozen.
Add winter squash chunks to soups, stews, or curries for a delicious autumn flavour. You can blend or process thawed winter squash chunks into a smooth purée or use your pre-made purée in baking items such as cakes, muffins, breads, or desserts. Purée is also delicious added to waffles, pancakes, risotto, and ravioli filling, or made into pasta sauce.

CANNING YOUR WINTER SQUASH

You can preserve blanched winter squash chunks through **pressure canning.** (Do *not* can squash purée; it is hazardous.) Peel the skin, scrape away seeds, and cut flesh into cubes. Blanch in boiling water (2 min) before packing into jars. Pressure canning steps, pg 57
Processing time: 55 min (pints) 90 min (quarts)

DEHYDRATING YOUR WINTER SQUASH

Winter squash takes around 6-12 hours to dehydrate, depending on the thickness of the pieces. To prevent discoloration, soak the squash pieces in a solution of 1 tablespoon of lemon juice per 4 cups water for five minutes first. Dehydrating steps, pg 63

TO USE: Add dehydrated squash to casseroles or stuffing for a burst of flavour. Add to homemade trail mix for a unique twist. Soak dehydrated winter squash in **warm water** for 15-20 minutes to rehydrate and use in soups, stews, curries, or risotto.

PICKLING YOUR WINTER SQUASH

Winter squash can be plain pickled or flavoured in any number of sweet or savoury pickle variations (such as sweet + spicy pickled, mustard seed pickled, apple cider pickled) to enjoy throughout the year. Peel, seed it, and cut into desired-size pieces. Soft-skinned varieties don't need to be peeled first (delicata, carnival, sweet dumpling). Pickling steps, pg 80 or 81   **Processing time (water bath canning):20 min**

TO USE: Toss pickled winter squash cubes or slices into salads with mixed greens, nuts, and cheese for a burst of flavour. Add to grain bowls (quinoa, rice, or couscous) along with other veggies and proteins. Use it as a topping for tacos, burritos, tostadas, or nachos. Serve pickled winter squash alongside a cheese platter, or spread it on toasted baguette slices topped with goat cheese or ricotta for a flavorful crostini or bruschetta. Mix finely chopped pickled winter squash into hummus or other creamy dips, or create a winter squash relish with diced onions, tomatoes, and fresh herbs to serve alongside grilled meats or fish.

FERMENTING winter squash is not common practice. The dense, low-moisture nature of squash can make the fermentation process challenging.

ZUCCHINI

Cylindrical soft-skinned vegetable with dense, mellow flesh.
(aka. Courgette)

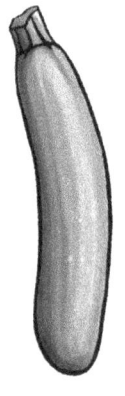
 Stems are edible when cooked, though often removed and discarded. The younger and fresher the zucchini, the more tender the stem is. You can leave stems attached when cooking or slice them off to sauté or roast on their own.

 With soft edible skin, these fellas can be sliced up and roasted, pan-fried, grilled, or added to your soups, stir fries, or pasta. They can also be shredded into baking or turned into zoodles (zucchini noodles) with a spiralizer.

FRESH STORAGE — Store unwashed on the counter if using within a few days, or in the refrigerator for longer (in a crisper drawer or paper bag) to allow for air circulation. Lasts 2 weeks.

QUICK TIP — Zucchini pairs well with meats and seafood, as well as ingredients like peppers, corn, basil, lemon, eggplant, garlic, onions, other summer squash, tomatoes, fresh herbs, nuts, cheeses (cheddar, parmesan, feta, ricotta), sour cream, and rice.

PRESERVATION — Freeze, dehydrate, ferment, or pickle.
(See next page for more)

FREEZING YOUR ZUCCHINI

You can freeze your zucchini raw, blanched, or cooked (pg 48).
Zucchini has a high water content, so freezing can make it mushy and watery. **Shred it if freezing raw** (for use in baking). **Blanch it if freezing slices or chunks** (for cooking). Be sure to drain any liquid after thawing, before using it in recipes, and plan for use in cooked or baked dishes only.

TO USE: Thaw in the refrigerator before cooking. Drain any liquid before using.
Toss frozen zucchini into soups, stews, chili, casseroles, lasagnas, or baked pasta dishes. Add to stir-fries, or sauté with herbs and other vegetables as a quick and easy side dish or addition to salads, grain bowls, or wraps. Use grated zucchini in baking recipes like zucchini bread, muffins, pancakes, or waffles.

CANNING It is not recommended to pressure can zucchini.

DEHYDRATING YOUR ZUCCHINI

Zucchini takes around 6-12 hours to dehydrate, depending on thickness of the slices. Slice thinly, shred or small dice. Dehydrating steps, pg 63

TO USE: Enjoy dehydrated zucchini chips as a crunchy, healthy snack. Rehydrate zucchini slices by soaking in hot water for 15-30 minutes. Add rehydrated zucchini to soups, stews, chili, casseroles, pasta dishes, omelets, or frittatas.

FERMENTING YOUR ZUCCHINI

Fermenting zucchini creates a probiotic-rich, tangy item that is delicious in salads, sandwiches, or as a side dish. Slice, chop, or cut into sticks. Fermenting steps, pg 74

TO USE: Enjoy fermented zucchini as classic pickles. Chop or slice and add it to salads, sandwiches, wraps, or grain bowls. Include on an antipasto platter. Chop fermented zucchini and mix it with tomatoes, onions, cilantro, and lime juice to create a unique and probiotic-rich zucchini salsa. Or toss it into cold noodle salad.

PICKLING YOUR ZUCCHINI

Zucchini can be plain pickled or flavoured in any number of sweet or savoury pickle variations (such as bread + butter pickled, taco-inspired pickled, maple dijon pickled) to enjoy throughout the year. Cut into rounds or spears. Pickling steps, pg 80 or 81
Processing time (water bath canning):10 min

TO USE: Pickled zucchini can be enjoyed as a side dish, a topping for salads, or a tangy snack. Include it in sandwiches, wraps, tacos or burritos for a burst of flavour. Create a relish by combining pickled zucchini with onions, bell peppers, and herbs to use as a condiment for burgers, hot dogs, or sandwiches. Add pickled zucchini to charcuterie boards to compliment cheeses, cured meats, and crackers. Top toasted bread with chopped, pickled zucchini, tomatoes, and fresh basil for a zesty bruschetta. Add it to grain bowls, buddha bowls, or cold noodle salads. Serve as a side dish for grilled meats or barbecue.

SEEDS

Vegetables // grown for their seeds

CORN

—

Starchy vegetable with sweet, juicy kernels covered by a husk.

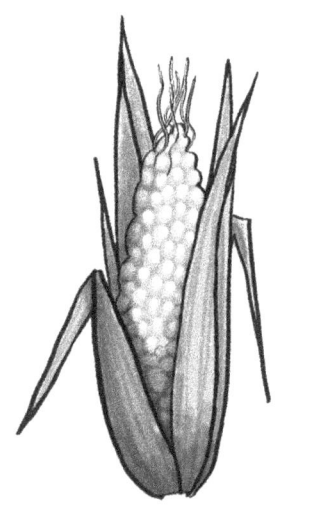

← Silks (glossy threads) are often discarded, but are edible. Generally used to make tea, or chopped and sprinkled over food— they can be dehydrated and ground into powder which stores up to a year.

← Kernels are deliciously edible both raw and cooked. They can be eaten right off the cob (grilled, boiled, or microwaved) or cut from the cob using a sharp knife sliding down along the cob. Add corn to salads, dips, or soups.

← Husks are inedible, but they serve the valuable purpose of keeping the corn moist and juicy until ready to eat. Sometimes left on during cooking (grilling or fire roasting) to trap in moisture, then removed before serving. Once removed, there are some creative uses for them— dry them for crafts (make wreaths or corn husk dolls), use for firestarter, or to steam fish or make tamales.

FRESH STORAGE	Corn is best eaten fresh or within the first couple of days. Leave husks on (to retain moisture); store cobs in the refrigerator in a plastic bag or sealed container up to 5 days.
QUICK TIPS	The easiest way to shuck corn is using a microwave. Cut the stalk end off the corn and microwave for 30 seconds to a minute. Using a towel or oven mitts, hold onto the silks end and squeeze the corn out of the husk like you would a tube of toothpaste.
	The easiest way to slice kernels from the cob is with a sturdy bundt pan. Prop the stem end in the centre hole and cut the kernels using a sharp knife, sliding down along the cob to fall directly into the pan for more ease and less mess.
PRESERVATION	Freeze, pressure can, dehydrate, ferment, or pickle. (See next page for more)

FREEZING YOUR CORN

You can freeze your corn raw, blanched, or cooked (pg 48).
You can freeze whole corn cobs or just the kernels. Slicing the kernels from the cob saves storage space and makes it easy to use in recipes. Freezing whole cobs allows for delicious corn on the cob, even in the off-season.
To freeze whole cobs: Remove the stems, leave the husks on (peeling away only the outermost layers), trim a full inch off both ends of each cob, then put them straight into freezer bags and freeze.
To freeze kernels: Remove husks and silks. Blanch cob (optional). Hold the cob upright and slice the kernels from the cob using a sharp knife sliding down along the cob. (If you have a sturdy bundt pan, prop the stem end in the centre hole and slice the kernels down so they fall directly into the pan for more ease and less mess.) Seal kernels in a freezer bag to freeze.

TO USE: Can cook directly from frozen.
Steam or microwave the frozen corn kernels and toss with a bit of butter, salt, and pepper for a simple and tasty side. Add to soups, stews, chili, casseroles, fried rice, tacos or dips. For frozen whole cobs, run them under warm water to remove the husks and silks. Then boil, steam, microwave, or wrap in aluminum foil and put on the grill.

DEHYDRATING YOUR CORN

Corn kernels take around 6-12 hours to dehydrate. Slice fresh kernels from cob. Blanch for 2 minutes. Dehydrating steps, pg 63

TO USE: Soak dehydrated corn kernels in water for a few hours, or cook it directly in dishes that have enough liquid, to rehydrate it. Use in soups, stews, chili, casseroles, fried rice, tacos, dips, or add to cornbread or muffin batter.

CANNING YOUR CORN

You can preserve raw corn through **pressure canning** for use in your favourite recipes or as a side. Cut the kernels off the cob and fill sterilized jars (leaving 1" of headspace). Pressure canning steps, pg 57   **Processing time: 55 min (pints) 85 min (quarts)**

FERMENTING YOUR CORN

Fermenting corn is less common, but it is possible. Experiment with the fermentation time and the addition of herbs and spices to create a unique flavour profile. Fermenting steps, pg 74

TO USE: Incorporate fermented corn into salsas or relishes. Add to grain bowls, tacos, or burritos. Mix fermented corn with cooked beans, diced tomatoes, and a light vinaigrette for a refreshing and tangy bean salad. Top grilled fish or seafood with a spoonful of fermented corn salsa for added flavour.

PICKLING YOUR CORN

Corn can be plain pickled or flavoured in any number of sweet or savoury pickle variations (such as spicy pickled, italian herb pickled, citrus pickled) to enjoy throughout the year. Pickling steps, pg 80 or 81   **Processing time (water bath canning):15 min**

TO USE: Toss pickled corn into green salads or grain bowls for a burst of tangy flavour. It pairs well with mixed greens, tomatoes, avocados, and your favourite dressing. Use as a topping for tacos, burritos, hot dogs, or wraps. Serve pickled corn alongside grilled or pan-seared fish or seafood. Sprinkle on top of omelets, frittatas, or scrambled eggs for a tangy and vibrant addition. Mix pickled corn into rice or grain salads for a unique flavour, or combine it with herbs, roasted vegetables, and a light vinaigrette.

FAVA BEANS

—

Creamy textured seeds with buttery taste.
(aka. Broad Beans)

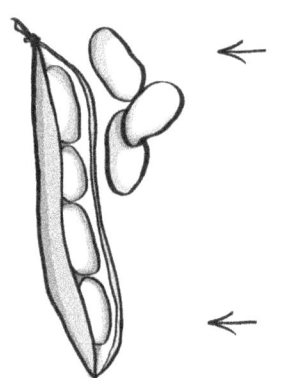

← Beans can be eaten raw or cooked. They are typically prepared by blanching (add them to salted boiling water for a few minutes until soft and bright green, then plunged into cold water to stop the cooking). If desired, gently remove the outer layer of waxy skin. Serve in salads, soups, with fish, mash onto toast (like avocado toast), or drizzle with olive oil, lemon juice, salt + pepper for a tasty standalone side dish.

← Spongey pods are inedible. Slip the pod open into two halves and slide your thumb down them to push the beans out. Discard pods.

FRESH STORAGE — Keep beans in their pods (to retain moisture), unwashed, in a plastic bag or sealed container in the refrigerator. Lasts up to 2 weeks. Shelled beans will only last a couple of days stored in the refrigerator.

QUICK TIP — Fava beans pair well with ingredients like lemon, mint, dill, feta, ricotta, parmesan, garlic, fresh herbs, bacon, smoked meats, pine nuts, fennel, asparagus, and peas.

PRESERVATION — Freeze, pressure can, dehydrate, ferment, or pickle.
(See next page for more)

FREEZING YOUR FAVA BEANS

You can freeze your fava beans blanched or cooked. You want to remove the outer skin before freezing for ease of use later on. Remove the beans from the pods. Blanch them (pg 48), then gently remove the outer layer of waxy skin before freezing.

TO USE: Can cook directly from frozen.
Sauté thawed fava beans with garlic, herbs, and a splash of lemon juice for a quick and tasty side dish, or mash them with garlic, olive oil, and lemon juice for a flavorful alternative to mashed potatoes. Purée fava beans to create a creamy dip or spread. Add thawed fava beans to a creamy risotto during the last few minutes of cooking, stir in fresh herbs like parsley or mint for added flavour. Add to soups, stews, pasta dishes, tacos, wraps, casseroles, or curries.

CANNING YOUR FAVA BEANS

You can preserve fresh fava beans through **pressure canning** for use in your favourite recipes or as a side. Remove from pods. Blanch them first (pg 48) and gently remove the outer layer of waxy skin before packing them into jars. Pressure canning steps, pg 57
Processing time: 40 min (pints) 50 min (quarts)

DEHYDRATING YOUR FAVA BEANS

It is usually recommended to let the fava pods dehydrate on the bushes. However, you can dry them like your other vegetables. Fava beans take around 8-12 hours to dehydrate. Shell them and discard pods. Blanch beans (pg 48) so the waxy outer skins can be easily peeled off). Dehydrating steps, pg 63

TO USE: Enjoy dehydrated fava beans as a crunchy and nutritious snack; season them with your favourite spices or eat them as is. To rehydrate, soak in water 8 to 12 hours or overnight. Use rehydrated fava beans in soups, stews, salads, pasta dishes, grain bowls, casseroles, fried rice, or curries.

FERMENTING YOUR FAVA BEANS

Fermenting fava beans creates a probiotic-rich, tangy condiment that can be used in salads, as a snack, or as a side dish. Remove from pods. Blanch (pg 48) and gently remove the outer layer of waxy skin before packing into jars. Fermenting steps, pg 74

TO USE: Toss fermented fava beans into salads; they pair well with fresh greens, tomatoes, cucumbers, and a simple vinaigrette. Add to grain bowls or buddha bowls. Incorporate into wraps, pasta dishes, or top roasted vegetables with fermented fava beans to add depth of flavour and a satisfying crunch.

PICKLING YOUR FAVA BEANS

Fava beans can be plain pickled or flavoured in any number of sweet or savoury pickle variations (such as sweet + tangy pickled, herb pickled, spicy pickled) to enjoy throughout the year. Remove from pods. Blanch and gently remove the outer layer of waxy skin before packing into jars. Pickling steps, pg 80 or 81
Processing time (water bath canning):10 min

TO USE: Pickled fava beans are a tasty snack enjoyed straight from the jar, served alongside charcuterie or cheese boards, or for adding a delicious zing to salads. Spread ricotta or goat cheese on crostini or bruschetta and top with pickled fava beans for a simple and elegant appetizer. Add them to rice or grain bowls. Blend pickled fava beans into a dip or spread with ingredients like garlic, olive oil, and lemon juice, and serve with pita or crackers.

PEAS

Round green seeds with sweet, grassy flavour.

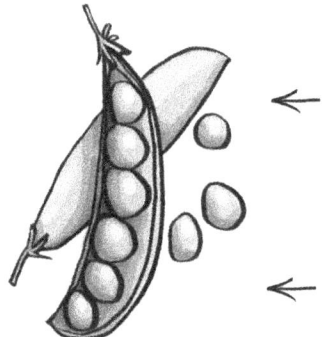

← Fresh peas are sweet and tender and can be enjoyed raw (straight from the pod) or cooked. Slip the pod open into two halves and slide your thumb down them to push the peas out. They can be steamed, boiled, served in warm salads, or stirred into a hot dish like risotto or pasta.

← Pods are fibrous and not typically eaten. However, they can be juiced (or boiled, blended, and passed through a sieve to make a tasty, vibrant juice) which can be consumed or stirred into risottos or soups for delicious flavour.

FRESH STORAGE — Keep peas in their pods (to retain moisture). Store in a plastic bag or sealed container in the refrigerator. Lasts up to 2 weeks. Shelled peas should be eaten right away or blanched and frozen.

QUICK TIP — Fresh peas pair well with ingredients like lemon, mint, dill, parsley, ricotta, parmesan, asparagus, potato, nuts, bacon, prosciutto, ham, pasta, and rice.

PRESERVATION — Freeze, pressure can, dehydrate, ferment, or pickle.
(See next page for more)

FREEZING YOUR PEAS

You can freeze your peas blanched or cooked (pg 48).
Remove peas from their pods before freezing.

TO USE: Can cook directly from frozen.
Add frozen peas to soups, stews, casseroles, pasta dishes, fried rice, pot pies, or curries. Incorporate frozen peas into a classic risotto for a burst of colour and a slightly sweet flavour. Steam or microwave frozen peas and serve them as a simple and nutritious side dish, add a touch of butter or herbs for extra flavour.

CANNING YOUR PEAS

You can preserve shelled peas through **pressure canning** for use in your favourite recipes or as a side. Fill jars with raw shelled peas (leaving 1" headspace). Pressure canning steps, pg 57 **Processing time: 40 min (pints or quarts)**

DEHYDRATING YOUR PEAS

Peas take around 4-10 hours to dehydrate, depending on their size and moisture content. Remove from pods. Blanch 1 minute. You can also season peas before dehydrating by tossing them with your favourite herbs or spices. Dehydrating steps, pg 63

TO USE: Enjoy dehydrated peas as a crunchy snack. Add them to soups, stews, casseroles, pasta dishes, fried rice, pot pies, or curries. Rehydrate peas by soaking them in hot water for 15 minutes, until they become plump and tender, to use in your favourite recipes.

PICKLING YOUR PEAS

Peas can be plain pickled or flavoured in any number of pickle variations (such as dill pickled, garlic pickled, mustard pickled) to enjoy throughout the year. Pickling steps, pg 80 or 81   **Processing time (water bath canning):15 min**

TO USE: Toss pickled peas into green salads, pasta salads, or grain salads for an added burst of flavour and crunch. Sprinkle pickled peas on top of grain bowls, such as quinoa or rice bowls, for a pop of flavour and colour. Use in asian-inspired dishes like fried rice or noodle bowls. Use as a garnish for cocktails, especially those with a savoury or herbal profile. Mix into egg salad or tuna salad for a tangy and crunchy addition. Serve as a side dish alongside grilled meats, roasted chicken, or fish.

FERMENTING YOUR PEAS

Fermenting peas is less common, but it is possible. You can experiment with it for use in salads, grain bowls, or as a side dish. Fermenting steps, pg 74

SNOW PEAS

—

Flat edible pods with soft seeds and crunchy, sweet flavour.

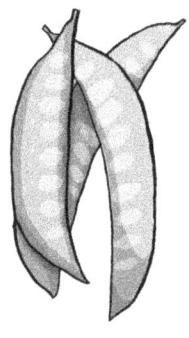

← Trim off the tough stem, or snap off the stem and pull the fibrous string off down the length of the pod. Discard.

← Whole pods can be enjoyed raw or gently cooked. Try quick grilling, pan-frying, or roasting them. They are also a delicious addition to salads, stir fries, or ramen.

FRESH STORAGE	Best enjoyed fresh, these are sweetest right after picking. Store unwashed in a perforated plastic bag or container in the refrigerator. Lasts a week.
QUICK TIP	Snow peas pair well with chicken, shrimp, beef, and pork, as well as ingredients like lemon, mint, basil, ginger, garlic, parmesan, sesame oil, asparagus, nuts, noodles, and rice.
PRESERVATION	Freeze, pressure can, dehydrate, ferment, or pickle. (See next page for more)

FREEZING YOUR SNOW PEAS

You can freeze your snow peas raw, blanched, or cooked (pg 48).
Freeze them whole or chopped, depending on your purpose. Trim ends and remove strings from the pods first. **Blanching is recommended** to improve texture and flavour. Keep in mind that the texture will be softer once thawed, so they are best used in cooked dishes.

TO USE: Can cook directly from frozen.
Add frozen snow peas to soups, stews, pasta dishes, fried rice, and stir fries-- **toss in during the last few minutes of cooking** to help maintain their crunch. Steam or sauté as a simple side dish, seasoned with a bit of salt, pepper, and perhaps a drizzle of olive oil, ginger, or just a splash of soy sauce for extra flavour. Sauté with other frozen vegetables to create a quick and easy vegetable medley, adding garlic and herbs.

CANNING YOUR SNOW PEAS

You can preserve snow peas through **pressure canning,** although it is not a common way to preserve them. Trim ends and remove strings from the pods first. Fill jars with raw snow peas (leaving 1" headspace). Pressure canning steps, pg 57
Processing time: 40 min (pints or quarts)

DEHYDRATING YOUR SNOW PEAS

Snow peas take 6-12 hours to dehydrate, depending on their size and moisture content. Trim ends and remove strings from the pods first. Blanch 1 minute. Dehydrating steps, pg 63

TO USE: To rehydrate, soak dehydrated snow peas in warm water for a few minutes until they plump up. You can also incorporate them directly into recipes that involve cooking or simmering, such as soups, stews, or casseroles. Add rehydrated snow peas to stir fries, curries, or grain bowls.

FERMENTING YOUR SNOW PEAS

Fermented snow peas can be enjoyed as a flavorful, probiotic-rich snack or added to your favourite dishes. Trim ends and remove strings from the pods first. Fermenting steps, pg 74

TO USE: Add to green or grain salads. Add to sandwiches or wraps for an extra layer of flavour. Roll fermented snow peas into spring or summer rolls with other fresh vegetables, tofu, or noodles. Top your grain bowls with fermented snow peas for a flavorful, probiotic boost. Serve as a side dish with grilled or roasted meats. Chop fermented snow peas and mix them with diced onions, tomatoes, and fresh herbs to create a flavorful relish for burgers or grilled vegetables.

PICKLING YOUR SNOW PEAS

Snow peas can be plain pickled or flavoured in any number of sweet or savoury pickle variations (such as soy ginger sesame pickled, tarragon pickled, mint pickled) to enjoy throughout the year. Trim ends and remove strings from the pods first. Pickling steps, pg 80 or 81 **Processing time (water bath canning):10 min**

TO USE: Enjoy pickled snow peas as a tasty pantry snack, or add to salads, sandwiches or wraps. Add to appetizer platters alongside cheeses, crackers, and cured meats. Use as a topping for Asian-inspired dishes like rice bowls, noodle dishes, or sushi rolls. Incorporate into tacos or burritos for a tangy and crisp component. Use as a garnish for seafood dishes, such as grilled fish or shrimp, or add to cold noodle salads for added zing and crunch. Use pickled snow peas as a filling for spring or summer rolls, along with other fresh vegetables and proteins. Use as a garnish for cocktails or mocktails.

STRING BEANS

Long edible pods with fibrous, grassy taste.

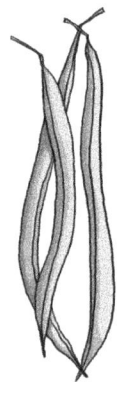

← Trim off stem and discard.

← Pod is snappy and delicious with a sweet fibrous crunch. Beans are best eaten cooked (in fact, you shouldn't consume large amounts of them raw). They are delicious steamed, sauteed, or roasted as a side dish or cooked in a stirfry.

FRESH STORAGE	Store unwashed in a plastic bag or sealed container in the refrigerator. Lasts up to 2 weeks.
QUICK TIP	String beans pair well chicken, shrimp, beef, pork, and ingredients like butter, parsley, dill, garlic, shallots, potatoes, bacon, almond, ginger, tarragon, and parmesan.
PRESERVATION	Freeze, pressure can, dehydrate, ferment, or pickle. (See next page for more)

FREEZING YOUR STRING BEANS

You can freeze your string beans blanched or cooked (pg 48).
Freeze them whole or chopped, depending on your purpose. Trim ends and remove any strings first. **Blanching is crucial to improve texture and flavour.** Keep in mind that the texture will be softer once thawed, so they are best used in cooked dishes.

TO USE: Can cook directly from frozen.
Add frozen string beans to soups, stews, fried rice, or stir fries. Incorporate into casseroles like green bean casserole. Steam or boil frozen green beans and toss them with a bit of butter, garlic, or lemon juice for a simple and flavorful side dish. Combine with other frozen vegetables to create a medley and season with herbs and spices for added flavour. Roast frozen green beans on a sheet pan along with other vegetables and your choice of protein for an easy one-pan meal.

CANNING YOUR STRING BEANS

You can preserve string beans through **pressure canning** for use in soups, casseroles, or in your favourite bean recipes. Trim ends. Use whole or chopped. Pressure canning steps, pg 57   **Processing time: 20 min (pints); 25 min (quarts)**

DEHYDRATING YOUR STRING BEANS

String beans take around 6-12 hours to dehydrate, depending on their size. Trim stems. Blanch 2 minutes. Dehydrating steps, pg 63

TO USE: To rehydrate, soak them in water for a few hours or overnight before cooking. Add rehydrated beans to soups, stews, casseroles, stir fries, fried rice, chili, or curry. Sauté rehydrated green beans with garlic, olive oil, and your favourite herbs for a simple side.

FERMENTING YOUR STRING BEANS

Fermented string beans are a probiotic-rich, tangy snack that can be used in salads, or as a topper or side to your favourite dishes. Trim ends. Leave whole or chop as desired. Fermenting steps, pg 74

TO USE: Enjoy fermented green beans as a crunchy, flavourful snack straight from the jar. Include them on an appetizer plate, on a charcuterie board, in salads, or as a topper on rice or grain bowls. Mix fermented green beans into pasta salads to provide a tangy contrast. Or use them as a creative cocktail garnish for drinks like Bloody Marys.

PICKLING YOUR STRING BEANS

Pickled string beans, often called "dilly beans", can be flavoured in any number of pickle variations (such as honey mustard pickled, zesty lemon pickled, spicy pickled) to enjoy throughout the year. Trim ends. Leave whole or chop as desired. Pickling steps, pg 80 or 81
Processing time (water bath canning):10 min

TO USE: Dilly beans are a delicious pantry treat enjoyed straight from the jar, served alongside charcuterie boards or cheese platters, or used as a garnish for Bloody Mary cocktails. They can also be used as a unique topping for hot dogs or burgers or added to pasta salads, green salads, or grain salads.

SUGAR SNAP PEAS
—

Crunchy, plump pods with sweet, juicy flavour.

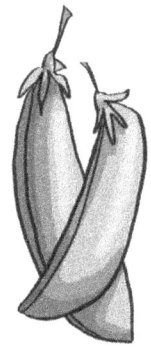

 Trim off the tough stem, or snap off the stem end and pull the fibrous string off down the length of the pod. Discard.

 Pods are best eaten whole (unopened), either raw or gently cooked so they don't lose their sweet crunch. Try quick grilling, pan-frying, or roasting them. They are delicious as a snack, in salads, or sliced into slivers over ramen.

FRESH STORAGE — These are best enjoyed fresh, and they are sweetest right after picking. Store unwashed in a perforated plastic bag or container in the refrigerator. Lasts a week.

QUICK TIP — Sugar snap peas pair well with chicken and shrimp, and ingredients like mint, lemon, shallots, sesame oil, garlic, ginger, soy sauce, sesame seeds, noodles, carrots, asparagus, and radishes.

PRESERVATION — Freeze, pressure can, dehydrate, ferment, or pickle.
(See next page for more)

FREEZING YOUR SUGAR SNAP PEAS

You can freeze your sugar snap peas raw, blanched, or cooked (pg 48).
Freeze them whole or chopped, depending on your purpose. Trim ends and remove any strings first. **Blanching is generally recommended** for the best texture and flavour.

TO USE: Can cook directly from frozen.
Add frozen sugar snap peas directly to a hot wok or skillet with other stir-fry ingredients. They cook quickly and maintain a crisp texture. You can also sauté frozen sugar snap peas in olive oil or butter with garlic, herbs, and a pinch of salt as a side dish to enjoy their natural sweetness. Steam frozen sugar snap peas for a few minutes until they are tender but still have a slight crunch. Toss with a vinaigrette for a refreshing salad.

CANNING YOUR SUGAR SNAP PEAS

You can preserve sugar snap peas through **pressure canning,** although it is not a common way to preserve them. If you do, trim ends and remove strings from the pods first. Pack raw pods into jars (leaving 1" headspace). Pressure canning steps, pg 57
Processing time: 40 min (pints or quarts)

DEHYDRATING SUGAR SNAP PEAS

Sugar snap peas take around 6-12 hours to dehydrate, depending on their size and moisture content. Trim ends and remove strings from the pods first. Blanch 1 minute. You can toss with seasonings to add flavor before dehydrating. Dehydrating steps, pg 63

TO USE: Enjoy dehydrated sugar snap peas as a standalone snack, or crush them into a powder for a flavorful seasoning. Create your own savoury snack mix by combining dehydrated sugar snap peas with pretzels, crackers, and other crunchy elements and seasoning with your favourite herbs and spices. Rehydrate by soaking them in warm water for 15-20 minutes before tossing them into salads, rice or grain bowls, stir fries, or casseroles.

FERMENTING YOUR SUGAR SNAP PEAS

Fermenting sugar snap peas creates a probiotic-rich, tangy snack or side dish. Trim ends and remove strings from the pods first. Fermenting steps, pg 74

TO USE: Toss fermented sugar snap peas into salads for an extra burst of flavour and crunch; they pair well with fresh greens, tomatoes, and a simple vinaigrette. Add to your charcuterie or appetizer boards. Add fermented sugar snap peas to stir-fries for a tangy kick (incorporate them toward the end of cooking to preserve their crunchiness). Top your grain bowls, or use as a garnish for various dishes, adding a pop of colour and tangy flavour to soups or even breakfast items like scrambled eggs.

PICKLING YOUR SUGAR SNAP PEAS

Sugar snap peas can be plain pickled or flavoured in any number of sweet or savoury pickle variations (such as sweet + tangy pickled, honey mustard pickled, lemon herb pickled) to enjoy throughout the year. Trim ends and remove strings from the pods first. Pickling steps, pg 80 or 81   **Processing time (water bath canning):15 min**

TO USE: Enjoy pickled sugar snap peas as a tangy and crunchy snack straight from the jar. Add to your charcuterie or appetizer boards. Add to rice bowls, noodle bowls, or grain bowls to add acidity and crunch. Use as a garnish for cocktails. Mix chopped pickled sugar snap peas into egg or chicken salad for added crunch and flavour.

GROWING FORWARD

As you leave off here, I hope you too have discovered that there is something truly magical about earthy, delicious vegetables. Their taste connects us back to the rich earth they sprouted from. Their textures and sensations take us on an edible journey from the moment they are in our hands. Looking upon them reminds us of all the beauty and vibrance of the natural world. They leave us invigorated, connected, and nourished whenever we consume them. Vegetables are a true treasure, and in having them one can't help but feel wealthy. Delight in those veggies!

I'm so glad you joined me on this walk from the garden to the dinner table. I hope you are inspired to eat fresh grown and feel more equipped to use, store, and maximize a beautiful array of vegetables for you and your loved ones. From the first snap of those crunchy carrots to the sweet pop of a pea, may your life be enriched with veggie goodness, reaping the health, well-being, and vitality of earth's delicious bounty!

With love,

Andrea

VEGETABLE INDEX

Acorn Squash............278
Arugula..................176
Asparagus..............134
Aubergine.............250
Basil......................184
Beets......................92
Beans....................306
Bok Choy...............138
Blue Hubbard..........278
Broccoli..................226
Broccolini.......(see broccoli)
Brussels Sprouts........230
Broad Beans............294
Buttercup...............278
Butternut................278
Cabbage.................234
Carrots...................98
Caraflex.................234
Cauliflower............238
Celeriac..................102
Celery....................142
Chard....................206
Chives...................184
Cilantro.................184
Collard Greens..........180
Corn......................290
Courgette...............284
Crookneck..............270
Cucumber..............246
Daikon...........(see radishes)
Delicata..................278
Dill.......................184
Eggplant................250
Endive...................188
Fava Beans..............294
Festival..................278
Fennel...................146
Garlic....................214
Garlic Scapes............150

Gem Squash.............254
Gold Zucchini.............270
Golden Nugget............278
Green Onions.............170
Herbs....................184
Kabocha.................278
Kale......................192
Kohlrabi.................154
Leeks....................158
Lettuce..................196
Lovage...................184
Microgreens.............210
Mizuna..............(see arugula)
Mustard Greens (see spinach)
Onions....................218
Oregano.................184
Pak Choi.................162
Parsley..................184
Parsnip..................106
Pattypan................270
Peas.....................298
Peppers..................258
Potatoes................110
Pumpkin.................262
Radicchio...............198
Radishes................116
Rhubarb.................166
Romanesco..............242
Round Zucchini..........268
Rosemary................184
Rutabaga................120
Sage.....................184
Salad Mix.............(see lettuce)
Savoy Cabbage..........234
Scallions................170
Shallots.................222
Snow Peas..............302
Sorrel..............(see spinach)
Spaghetti Squash........278

Spinach..................202
Squash..................278
Straightneck............270
String Beans............306
Sugar Snap Peas..........310
Summer Squash..........270
Sunburst.................270
Sweet Dumpling.........278
Sweet Potato............124
Swiss Chard.............206
Thyme..................184
Tomatoes................272
Turnips..................128
Vegetable Marrow.........284
Watercress..........(see arugula)
Winter Squash..............278
Yam..............see page 126
Zucchini..................284

ABOUT THE AUTHOR

Andrea Kristin lives in the Central Alberta prairies with her husband and children on their organic market garden farm affectionately known as Grey Arrow Farm (@greyarrowfarm). Every summer they feed local families in their community delicious vegetables through their CSA program. She loves to write, paint, and photograph. She enjoys good food and taking in the beauty of this wild world.

www.ingramcontent.com/pod-product-compliance
Lightning Source LLC
Chambersburg PA
CBHW041035020526
44118CB00043BA/2949